Hanging On and Letting Go:

The Art of Real Delegation

Hanging On and Letting Go:

The Art of Real Delegation

TOM MCCONALOGUE

BLACKHALL
Publishing

This book was typeset by ARK Imaging for

BLACKHALL PUBLISHING
33 Carysfort Avenue
Blackrock
Co. Dublin
Ireland

e-mail: info@blackhallpublishing.com
www.blackhallpublishing.com

© Tom McConalogue, 2008

ISBN: 978-1-84218-119-5

A catalogue record for this book is available from the British Library.

All rights reserved. No part of this publication may be reproduced, stored in a retrieval system or transmitted in any form or by any means, electronic, mechanical, photocopying, recording or otherwise, without the prior, written permission of the publisher.

This book is sold subject to the condition that it shall not, by way of trade or otherwise, be lent, resold, hired out, or otherwise circulated without the publisher's prior consent in any form of binding or cover other than that in which it is published and without a similar condition including this condition being imposed on the subsequent purchaser.

Printed in Ireland by ColourBooks Ltd

About the Author

Tom is an independent consultant working in the areas of personal skills and change management. His early career was in human resources before he joined the Irish Management Institute where he ran management development programmes and worked with organisations on improving their competencies and approaches to change.

His latter career has involved him mainly as an Organisation Development (OD) consultant working with groups and organisations managing their own changes in participative ways. He has a Masters degree in Organisation Development and a Ph.D. in Change Management.

Tom has written many articles and several books, including *Eat the Elephants and Fight the Ants* (Blackhall Publishing, 2003) on the subject of personal effectiveness and time management and *Dealing with Change: Lessons for Irish Managers* (Oak Tree Press, 2003). He continues to work as a trainer and consultant.

Tom can be contacted at:

Tom McConalogue and Associates
32 Burlington Gardens
Dublin 4
e-mail: mcconalt@clubi.ie
web: www.tommcconalogue.com

Table of Contents

Preface — xi

Acknowledgements — xiii

Chapter 1 – Letting Go of Real Responsibility — 1
Broaden the Delegation Options — 3
Focus on the Big Picture — 5
Share the Real Challenges — 8
Give People Response–Ability — 9

Chapter 2 – Starting Delegation with Yourself — 19
Energise Your Vision — 20
Keep the Main Things Main — 23
Manage the Priorities into Action — 25
Renew Your Leadership Style — 27

Chapter 3 – Challenging People to Perform — 37
Make Clear Demands on Your Staff — 38
Agree Mutual Goals — 39
Group Goal-Setting and Review (GGSR) — 42
Clarify Roles and Activities — 47

Chapter 4 – Coaching for Confidence — 53
Influence Staff through Active Listening — 55
Benefit from the Feedback Effect — 61
Deal with Defensive Behaviour — 65
Push Back the Monkeys — 68

Chapter 5 – Motivating Staff Beyond Expectations — 73
Symptoms and Causes of De-Motivation — 74
Practical Theories of Motivation — 75
The Power of Expectation — 86
Enrich Routine and Repetitive Work — 90

Chapter 6 – Building a Winning Team — 93
Less People – More in Teams — 93
Qualities of a Winning Team — 95
Use the Team to Improve Teamwork — 99
Encourage Team Talk — 101
Meetings as Microcosms — 102
Creative Ways to Improve Teamwork — 107

Chapter 7 – Dealing with Problem Staff — 113
Another View of Difficult People — 114
Strategies with Problem Staff — 115
Counsel the Cause — 116
Confront their Behaviour — 117
Cope with the Relationship — 123
Change the Job or Situation — 125
When to Start the Funeral — 128

Chapter 8 – Making Delegation Happen — 131
Schedule Time for Letting Go — 132
Keep Appointments with Yourself — 133
Institutionalise Contacts with Your Staff — 136
Practical Tools for Delegation — 144

Contents

Chapter 9 – What Real Delegators Do   **151**
Quality Time for Staff   153
Genuine Interest and Concern   154
Clear Demands and Tough Empathy   155
Corrective and Encouraging Feedback   156
Mainly Hands-Off Styles   157
Positive Regard and Respect   158
Pressing the Right Buttons   158
And Worst Bosses Too   162

References   **167**

Preface

If managing is all about getting things done through other people how is it that many managers end up doing so much themselves? How also is it that managers give so much time to the reactive and operational issues in the job there is often little time left for the more proactive and strategic challenges? And why is it that many managers with responsibility for ensuring quality, improving service or implementing new initiatives seem to be imposing their vision on a busy and uninterested workforce?

> *Delegation is about hanging on to what you want to let go of – responsibility*
> *And letting go of what you want to hang on to – control.*

Getting results through others is not just about giving people more things to do, it is about letting go of real responsibility, which means getting your staff to take personal ownership of the broader and more challenging tasks that are often not spelled out in detail. And managers only let go that degree of control if they trust their staff to show the same level of concern as they would themselves. Trust is critical to delegation. In the absence of trust you never really let go of responsibility, and yet how can you trust people if you are unwilling to let go?

As much an art as a science, delegation cannot be distilled into a neat set of principles. While some managers are blessed with skills or acquire them through early role models, for most it is a hard-earned competence. And, while there are techniques and approaches to getting the best out of others, you can't build trusting relationships unless you also make time to clarify what you want from your people, listen to their views, monitor what you give away, and recognise and reward them for their commitment and achievements.

In a practical way this book sets out to examine how managers can improve their delegation skills and where they need to focus their attention if they are to develop working relationships sufficient to let go of real responsibility to their staff. While suggesting they should start by looking at their own management functions and leadership style, the book examines a host of practical methods and techniques for managers who want to get the very best from their staff.

Acknowledgements

As with many books this has been influenced and supported by many friends and colleagues. I would like to pay special tribute to some of the early mentors in my career, including Neil McMeeking and Tony Carr at SGB who gave me early responsibility and the opportunity to learn from my mistakes, and Tom Boydell at Sheffield Polytechnic (now Hallam University) who introduced me to the joys of teamwork and having fun.

I would also like to acknowledge the contribution of many colleagues at the Irish Management Institute. Teaching and consulting are two of the best ways of developing your own organisational models and management practices, and working with colleagues on assignments is even more challenging. Also, I would like to recognise the contribution of those who worked with me in a supporting role over the years, including Patricia O'Kelly, Margaret Scally, Bairbre O'Kelly, Geraldine McDonnell, Carol Fitzpatrick and Margaret Maher, who in different ways helped to form my thinking on the subject matter of the book.

I am greatly indebted to Gerard O'Connor, Elizabeth Brennan and Eileen O'Brien of Blackhall Publishing for their always helpful advice and patience, and trusting me to deliver on this project. Thanks are also due in no small measure to my long-time colleague Ray Leonard for his onerous checking and most helpful comments on the manuscript.

Finally, I would like to thank my family for their continuing presence, especially my partner Verona for her unfailing encouragement and support, and my mother Lena who continues to be a guiding mentor by being herself.

CHAPTER 1

Letting Go of Real Responsibility

One of the major challenges for any manager today is how to get their people to deliver a superior day's work for a fair day's pay. Some leaders learn the value of preaching simple messages to get the best out of others. When Ronald Reagan, sometimes called 'the great communicator', was re-elected president for a second term, with a landslide majority, one reporter captured his style in these words: 'he knows the issues, he keeps them simple and he keeps repeating them.' In a similar way Thomas J. Watson created a proud and lasting culture for IBM, taking every opportunity to inspire others to share his commitment to customer service and respect for the individual. No one was left in any doubt that working for IBM was more than just a job.

Other managers adopt a tougher approach to getting things done through others, including the legendary J. Edgar Hoover who insisted on signing off on every decision, no matter how trivial. His staff were so fearful of making mistakes they rarely questioned his instructions even if they were unclear or ambiguous. One of the many anecdotes about Hoover concerned a draft memo he once received from a secretary where he thought the page margins were too small. He scrawled a warning in big red letters across the top: 'watch the borders'. Legend has it that next morning two hundred extra agents were assigned to the borders with Canada and Mexico.

Hanging On and Letting Go: The Art of Real Delegation

In contrast, reports of Richard Branson's approach to managing people often verged on reckless abandon. Apart from an outrageous sense of fun and celebration that included fancy dress days, impromptu fun breaks and throwing individuals into fountains, his willingness to delegate responsibility to people with no obvious qualifications or experience helped to create the culture of innovation and risk-taking that characterises Virgin to this day. By turning record packers into talent scouts, and magazine salesmen into managers, Branson was seen to be paying them the compliment of saying 'I trust you to do your best' and that trust, according to his many admirers, was more than repaid with commitment and loyalty. Likewise, Jack Welch, former CEO of General Electric (GE), sees trust as central to delegation. While the nickname 'Neutron Jack' was earned in the early days when he radically reduced the middle management bureaucracy that had been stifling staff at lower levels, he went on to build a performance culture that sustained the company through his twenty years at the helm. The leadership challenge, according to Welch, is convincing managers that their role is not to control people or stay on top of things, but to guide, energise and excite their staff about the future.

As the traditional command and control culture gives way in most organisations to flatter structures and closer relationships with customers and suppliers, the role of the manager in relation to their staff has changed. Organisations can no longer afford a compliant workforce and managers ruling by decree. Instead there is increasing need at all levels for people who are committed to service, teamwork, quality and innovation. The new paradigm has put a great deal of pressure on managers to work more closely with their staff and to trust them with shared responsibility which, for many who were schooled in hierarchical 'hands-on' styles, flies in the face of their natural desire to remain in control. But, whatever your preferred style, in one way or another real delegation is critical to getting the best out of others, and paradoxically

Letting Go of Real Responsibility

the only way to ensure that you also have time to achieve results in your own job.

BROADEN THE DELEGATION OPTIONS

Managers who complain about not having enough time for their major priorities usually have little problem identifying tasks they could and should be giving to others. One of the major blocks to letting go is that managers are inclined to see delegation as simply giving more work to staff who are often seen as already overworked. However, other choices begin to present themselves when delegation is viewed as a broader concept. In reality there are four places that managers can let go: firstly and most obviously by developing key staff to take on additional responsibilities, or at least refusing to accept their problems so easily. Secondly, most managers could push some of their work upwards by saying 'no' more often to things that are dumped on them from above or by others who may have assumed the right to shift their priorities. Thirdly, managers could get rid of some tasks by practising reverse delegation, which involves pushing things back to colleagues who may have come to see them as a convenient place to offload their problems.

Four places to let go:

1. Downwards by giving key staff more work and responsibility
2. Upwards by saying 'no' more often to things that are not part of your job
3. Sideways by pushing back problems and minor issues
4. Into the bin by giving less time to some things or not doing others at all

And finally, most managers could make better use of the waste paper basket as an elemental tool in delegation. The Law of Calculated Neglect, which counsels 'many things if left alone will simply go away', suggests the waste bin as one of the best places to delegate much of the routine and trivia that comes across the manager's desk each day (FIB – file it in the bin). As a keen observer of creeping bureaucracy in the civil service C. Northcote Parkinson concluded that 'work tends to expand to fill the time or number of staff to do it'. While the common response to an increasing workload is a demand for more staff, in reality, no matter how many people you have, they will all end up busy, and no matter how few staff, most of the work will still get done. Before assuming there is a need to increase staffing levels or extend overtime, examine the possibility that your workload could be reduced by giving some things less of your time or indeed not doing them at all. Part of any manager's job can be delegated by simply pushing it back to where it belongs, committing less time to some things, or saying 'no' to the unrealistic demands of others.

Table 1.1: How Many Hours Can You Let Go?

Delegate-able Tasks	Current Hours (weekly)	Delegate-able Hours (weekly)	Action
Answering queries from customers	4	2	Redirect more queries to Joan and Frank
Meetings with suppliers	3	2	Delegate two routine meetings to Harry
Travelling to branch offices	8	4	Replace by 50 per cent with e-mail, fax and weekly reports
Writing reports for head office	2	1	Systematise them and delegate part to Brian
Ad hoc meetings with boss	6	3	Say no to some and work at reducing time on others
Total	23	12	

Letting Go of Real Responsibility

One simple way to test your options for letting go is to draw up a list of the work-related activities you would like to give less of your time (see Table 1.1). How many hours does it amount to? Ask yourself the following questions about each activity:

1. How much time am I currently giving this task?
2. How much time is it worth?
3. How can I let go of this task, at least in part?

FOCUS ON THE BIG PICTURE

Apart from delegating more of your work as a way of easing the potential for over-commitment and stress, one of the main reasons for letting go to others is to find more time for the priorities on which you should be focusing. Managing is not just about doing things for today, it is also about doing things today to ensure the future of your area, which includes initiating, developing, changing and improving things. At all levels, managers are increasingly expected to be strategic and proactive as continuous improvement and change become the norm – yet it is important areas such as planning, thinking, coaching and training that often end up as casualties to work pressure and urgency.

> *On his appointment as Chancellor of the University of Cincinnati, following a successful career in academia, Warren Bennis saw a golden opportunity to put his management theories to the test. It wasn't long, however, before his aspirations for the university had become casualties to the sheer volume of minor issues and problems that came across his desk every day, each demanding an immediate response. Reflecting on that troubled period he recognised how he had become victim to an unwitting conspiracy that*

seemed designed to prevent him from doing anything to change the status quo in the university. It also dawned on him that many of the same colleagues who had shared his vision were part of a conspiracy aimed at ensuring that he would never have enough time to achieve anything of significance.[1]

Why is it that so many managers who see clear challenges in the job and identify with the need to be more proactive and strategic end up on a daily treadmill of activity and less than satisfied with the results they are achieving? Part of the reason is that managers deal with two very different types of work in their day, one of which has to do with handling operational routines like attending meetings, completing paperwork, dealing with problems and minor crises, and responding to a host of distractions from other people (see Table 1.2).

While these activities can take up a substantial part of their day, managers have little difficulty responding to them because

Table 1.2:   Reactive and Proactive Work

Reactive work (short-term/tangible/rewarding)	Proactive work (long-term/abstract/overwhelming)
– Routine meetings/paperwork, etc. – Handling minor problems – Responding to urgency – Dealing with interruptions ↓ **Usually Gets Done**	– Developing the business – Meeting objectives and targets – Focusing on key tasks, e.g. planning, staff development – Meeting deadlines on projects ↓ **Needs to be Made Happen**

Letting Go of Real Responsibility

they are part of their familiar routine, are generally short-term and tangible, and as such can be despatched in the timeframe available. Although they complain about the amount of routine and trivia in their day, managers also enjoy the cut and thrust of quick-fix problems, interruptions, correspondence and meetings and would feel denied if those things were absent. Wouldn't it be a dull old day if there were no e-mails, telephone interruptions, minor crises or meetings to attend? Be honest.

The main reasons for letting go to your staff:

- To make more time for the real challenges in your own job
- To reverse the tendency of doing too much yourself
- To share real responsibility with your staff
- To challenge, motivate and retain good staff

However, as well as the reactive and routine tasks in the job managers are also responsible for another type of work which includes developing their area of the business, focusing on key tasks such as planning, staff development, meeting deadlines and targets, and initiating and managing projects. Unlike reactive work, the activities that make up the proactive side of the manager's function are less tangible and the results are only seen in the longer-term. Consequently they are less attractive, hard to start or keep energy for, and as such tend to become the subject of procrastination and delay.

In an attempt to cope with the increasing demands in their day, many managers get caught in the balance between the operational side of the job and work that has to do with achieving results for the future. And while finding ways to let go some of the daily urgency and routine would seem the obvious answer, there is no guarantee it would lead to managers becoming any more effective – it may simply result in one set of routines and distractions being replaced by another. Letting go of routine and urgency to others also means finding ways to hang onto the strategic and long-term challenges in your own job.

SHARE THE REAL CHALLENGES

Organisations today, whether in the private or public sector, are becoming increasingly sensitive to the environments in which they operate, a major part of which is the customer or client and the competition. It has driven many businesses to focus more of their resources on broader concerns such as quality, service, innovation, delivery and friendliness and in many cases to see them as their main competitive advantage. Some years ago a group of consultants at McKinseys developed the 'Seven S's' model as a convenient framework for looking at the main categories that require attention in any organisation. The Seven S's include Strategy, Structure, Systems, Style, Shared Values, Skills and Staff. Follow-up studies by Peters and Waterman,[2] Collins and Porras,[3] and Pascale,[4] which used the McKinsey model as a framework for analysing business performance over a wide range of industries, identified the critical differences between the successful and less successful companies as mainly lying in the softer areas of Shared Values, Style, Skills and Staff (Table 1.3).

Table 1.3: The Seven S Framework

Strategy	
Structure	Hard S's
Systems	
Style	
Shared Values	Soft S's
Staff	
Skills	

Letting Go of Real Responsibility

While not minimising the importance of the hard S's, which are often driven from the top, most of the softer S's can only be fully realised if staff take ownership of their contribution towards making them happen. An important reason for any manager to pursue real delegation is that customer care, friendliness, teamwork or product quality cannot be unveiled and pushed through the organisation in the same way as a new piece of technology or a change in systems. Softer values and goals are only taken on board and owned by the staff when they are actively involved in the process of agreeing what they are and are committed to making them happen.

Although there may be compelling reasons for involving your staff in the broader challenges for the department or section there is also data to suggest that less than one in four people feel they are well utilised and working to their full potential. While part of the problem is that managers look for simplistic solutions, such as slogans and training, to complex issues like better service provision or quality improvement, they are also wedded to a view that most people do not want additional responsibility. A wealth of evidence shows not only that the combination of challenging work and opportunities for involvement and self-development is the greatest source of empowerment for staff but that managers have a major influence on creating the conditions in which staff are committed to giving of their best.

GIVE PEOPLE RESPONSE – ABILITY

The unwillingness of many managers to let go of real responsibility to their staff can be summed up in a word: 'TRUST'. The grand paradox in delegation is that if you don't trust your staff they will never develop the confidence to take on real responsibility, and yet how can you let go unless you trust them? In the same way that it would be foolish to let someone lower you over a cliff unless you were confident they could get you back, so it would be short-sighted to trust your staff with greater levels of responsibility if you see them as less than competent or confident about doing the job. Yet that is what delegation is all about – or is it?

> *The way to make people responsible*
> *Is to give them responsibility*

Central to the relationship between trust and letting go is a distinction between delegating work and responsibility. As the restaurant manager in a hotel, should you instruct one of the waiters to lay the tables for lunch, you are delegating work. Not only is the task clear but you retain a degree of control on how he or she does the job, either by checking the results or observing them. On the other hand if you ask one of your staff to organise the banqueting facilities for a major conference in two months time you are letting go of a more ambiguous task where you are less in control of the detail and their performance is more difficult to measure. Delegating that level of responsibility means you have to trust the person, and that takes time.

> *The critical difference between managing manual workers and knowledge workers, according to management guru Peter Drucker, is one of timeframe. 'One can say to a manual worker, "the standard calls for fifty pieces an hour and you are only turning out forty-two". One has to sit down with a knowledge worker and think through with him what should be done and why, before one can even know whether he is doing a satisfactory job or not.'* [5]

With an increasing focus by many organisations on critical areas like quality, service and delivery, workers are being asked to take more responsibility for what is less clear and controllable. And trusting people to deliver on that level of responsibility is not easy. Even

Letting Go of Real Responsibility

in close relationships we find it hard to let go to – typically we trust few people and we don't let go to those we don't trust. A quick examination of how we learn to develop trust in personal relationships offers some clues to building effective working relationships with staff.

With people we trust:

- We make time for them even when there isn't a need
- We share what we want from each other
- We listen to their needs and expect them to respond to ours
- We touch base frequently to find out how they are doing
- We help them create expectations of success rather than failure
- We reward their achievements and help them learn from their mistakes
- We share open and honest feedback as a way of strengthening the relationship

Building good relationships with your staff involves a similar process. Simply telling people to do things and expecting them to be done is fine when the job is simple, you can observe them and there are clear standards by which you can assess the results. However, building enough trust in the relationship to feel comfortable with letting go of complex and demanding tasks means making 'quality time' for the following:

1. Clarifying what is expected
2. Helping them take ownership
3. Providing support and encouragement
4. Rewarding them with recognition

Clarifying Expectations

Communicating what you want from your staff is different from telling them. One reason expectations between managers and staff often remain unclear is that managers frequently say what they don't mean and staff often accept what they don't understand. Have you ever read an article or listened to a speech that was confusing? The tendency is to blame yourself, at least in part. But perhaps the author was unclear, or that erudite speaker was less than prepared for his audience. Typically it is the recipient who gets blamed when there is misunderstanding in communications. How often have you heard managers say 'I explained it in detail and he still screwed it up'? Maybe it was clear in the manager's head but was badly expressed. And the manager's frustration at not getting instant commitment may have been all too clear to the subordinate.

What Chris Argyris calls 'defensive routines' also increases the possibility of confusion in relationships.[6] Although a manager may think he or she has communicated clearly what they want, the person may be confused about what they see as a mixed message such as, 'I want you to take responsibility, but if there are problems…', or, 'this is the number one priority, but don't let it get in the way of your other work'. No wonder people complain they are given responsibility but not authority. And when managers communicate mixed messages rarely do staff challenge their confusion, resulting in the issue further becoming 'undiscussable', where both parties pretend that things are clear when in fact they are not. Although they may be unclear about a task the typical response by most staff to 'do you understand what I am asking you to do?' is an almost involuntary 'yes, I think so'.

What you expect from your staff also bears repeating. Telling people once is seldom enough, as parents learn in trying to get children to make their beds or clean their shoes – you have to gently but firmly nag. Sometimes people genuinely don't hear the first time they are asked to take on a task because they are reading between the lines or are distracted by something more urgent on their desk. Have you ever experienced driving along a familiar route and not remembering whether you had passed a particular landmark or village? Although you may have been driving the car safely a part of your brain may have been working on something else. Sometimes it is important to get the other person's attention before briefing them on a complex task. It may mean choosing a time and place where the process won't be rushed or interrupted. It also helps if you repeat what has been agreed several times, summarising as you go along, and again at the end of the discussion. Additional ways of clarifying what you want may include putting it in writing, reminding them frequently or having regular progress reviews.

A great deal of the misunderstanding that occurs between managers and their staff can be traced to insufficient 'quality time' being given to clarifying expectations. And there is a wide discrepancy between the amount of time that managers think they give to explaining what they want and how their staff experience the same process. In a survey of over 200 employees, 43 per cent reported their managers rarely or only occasionally clarifying what they expected, while in the same survey over 52 per cent of their managers saw themselves as defining clear goals and objectives for their staff frequently or very frequently.[7]

Getting Acceptance

The aim of delegation is transferring ownership to the other person. If delegation is a one-way process then the other person doesn't have real ownership, and if things go wrong, they are blameless – 'it wasn't my idea' or 'I didn't agree to do it this way'. And there is a critical difference between agreeing to something and taking ownership, which only occurs when people feel committed and confident they will be supported in their efforts.

One of the most frustrating responses for managers when asking someone to take on a task is the 'head nodding' syndrome, where they think the other person has accepted but are left with the uneasy feeling that nothing is going to happen – and they are probably right. In their anxiety to delegate, managers sometimes overreact when they sense reluctance in their staff, and end up pushing them rather than dealing with their concerns. When people are less than willing to take ownership there is usually a good reason, and it may have less to do with the task than the process.

> *Recently I attended a meeting where a group of managers were being briefed by their boss on a change in work practices that they, in turn, had to communicate to their staff. Twenty minutes into the meeting the concerns of one or two managers were joined by others who expressed confusion and some hostility towards the changes. At a half-time coffee break I persuaded their boss to spend the second half of the meeting just listening to their concerns rather than pushing on with the agenda and to schedule another meeting in a week's time. It paid off. A week later the same managers met again, with much more willingness to take responsibility for implementing the changes.*

Sometimes the best way of encouraging people to take ownership is to listen. The simple act of asking questions and summarising back what you think you are hearing helps the person think through what he or she is being asked to do, and lets them know their input is valued – 'how long do you think it will take?', 'what are the options on this?' and 'what support will you need?' One of the major elements in what people see as the blind loyalty of Japanese workers is that they are listened to by their managers, the origin of consensual decision-making residing less in a compliant workforce than in managers spending more time in face-to-face dialogue with their staff than their Western counterparts.

Conversely, it is difficult for people to take real ownership if their boss is pushing them for action, and the feeling they are being forced into acceptance only adds to that anxiety. Simple

Letting Go of Real Responsibility

ways to check whether a person has taken ownership for a task includes getting him or her to summarise what has been agreed, suggesting dates by which the task, or stages of the task, will be completed, and confirming those commitments in writing. It may also help if you agree ways in which their progress will be monitored, whether at regular meetings or through reports or e-mails. And if what was agreed isn't happening, it is more than likely ownership was not taken in the first place, so look for other ways to get them to see the task as their own.

Monitoring and Supporting

Some managers are good at letting go to others but less consistent about following up. As a manager you never completely let go of responsibility – if things go wrong it is still your neck on the line. While it may involve a simple enquiry, such as 'how is that job going?' or 'have there been any more hold-ups?', monitoring serves both a checking and a rewarding function. Bosses do need to know what their people are doing, and staff do need to be reminded that their manager is interested in their progress.

> *People do what you inspect, not what you expect* –
> Louis Gerstner, ex-CEO of IBM

Another way to follow up on delegated tasks is to be available if there are problems or potential obstacles. But take care in responding that you don't take back what you have given away. It is all too easy to assume that when people ask for help they are looking for advice. If your staff want assistance it is often better to help them examine the options, support them on a particular course of action, or simply act as a sounding board. Sending them away with a solution to their problem at best satisfies the moment – at worst it may suggest that you are still holding onto responsibility.

Apart from casual contacts it can also be of benefit to regularise the monitoring process by blocking out a couple of half hours each week to do some managing by wandering around (MBWA) as a way of touching base with staff on specific tasks. Additionally, spending ten minutes a month with each person reviewing progress on their work or projects would only add an hour or two a week for most managers. Alternatively, hold weekly staff meetings to check on the status of delegated tasks and recognise the efforts of individuals in front of their peers. And if you don't get on well with some of your staff, don't leave monitoring to chance. Reverse the tendency to avoid them by initiating regular meetings until the relationship improves. At the beginning you may not find those contacts rewarding, and they may not either, but increasing the frequency of contact gives you an opportunity to repeat what you want from them and for them to feel their views and concerns are being heard.

Rewarding with Recognition

Much of what we do in life is motivated by the desire to please others, whether parents, spouses, teachers or bosses. And the recognition we receive is critical to our performance; as Ernst Dichter once said, 'people are more hungry for recognition than they are for food'. Ways in which managers can reward and recognise their staff include communicating high expectations, recognising their effort and results, and developing a climate where people want to perform.

Apart from providing general forms of recognition it is also important to reward people for the specific behaviours you want to encourage, whether to be more of a team player, get their reports in on time or to be more actively involved in a task group. Many managers get the best out of their people by using an intuitive or deliberate pattern of rewards called 'reinforcement'. Parents do it naturally with children, praising their spelling abilities, marvelling at their attempts to make a bed or cooing over their artwork, as a way of shaping their behaviour over time. We do it more subtly with family

Letting Go of Real Responsibility

members and close friends when we want to encourage them in a particular pursuit, change their personal appearance or reverse a bad habit. When it comes to motivating staff the simple 'Law of Effect' says a great deal in stating, 'things which are rewarded tend to be repeated and things that are unrewarded tend to be extinguished'; confirmed by one report in which 49 per cent of respondents identified recognition as the single most important reward in the job.

However, while they may value the importance of recognition in their personal lives, many managers are still wedded to the idea that the only way they can reward staff is with money. While not dismissing the importance of bonuses or accelerated increments as an inducement to join a company or to stay in the job, commentators such as Moss Kanter view the popular links between money and motivation as simplistic. In a study of the more innovating companies she found they relied very little on monetary incentives and rewards. Instead they created an abundance of mechanisms for praising and recognising the efforts and achievements of their staff, such as thank you notes, public pats on the back, celebration, award schemes, the invitation to join a task group, or being given a special assignment. She also found the more innovative companies shared a common belief – that it is the manager's job to make every person into a winner, not just the high flyers.[8]

While at a superficial level delegation can be viewed as a set of procedures aimed at getting staff to take on more work, in reality it is a much broader process for sharing responsibility and letting go of control. In developing trusting relationships there are no short cuts to letting your staff know again and again what you expect from them, supporting them in taking ownership, monitoring what you give away and rewarding individual and group effort. And you only let go to other people when there is a trusting relationship, and that means making quality time for staff. In the final analysis it is consistency of action more than inspiring words that convince others that the offer of shared responsibility is authentic and not just flavour of the month.

Complete the simple checklist in Table 1.4 as a way of checking your own commitment to real delegation:

Table 1.4: Delegating Responsibility

To get my staff to take on more responsibility...	Yes	Maybe	No
1. I need to spend more time clarifying the roles, tasks and authorities of my staff			
2. I need to be more certain that my staff understand what I want from them			
3. I need to be more available to listen to how my staff feel about what they are doing			
4. I need to spend time getting staff to take more ownership (be as committed as me) of their own responsibilities			
5. I need to check more frequently on the progress of tasks I have given to others			
6. I need to be more in touch with what my staff are doing (their work, concerns, needs) so I can support them			
7. I need to find more ways to recognise, reward and encourage the efforts of my staff			
8. I need to review the progress of my staff more frequently and give them feedback on how they are doing			

Analyse your commitment to delegation by adding together each pair of responses, i.e. 1+2, 3+4, 5+6 and 7+8. The four sets of responses reflect the extent to which you need to spend more time, 1. Clarifying expectations, 2. Getting acceptance, 3. Monitoring or 4. Rewarding your staff, as part of the process for encouraging them to take real responsibility for what they do.

CHAPTER 2

Starting Delegation with Yourself

While the obvious advice to any manager working under pressure is to find ways of sharing more of the workload with their staff, in reality we don't let go easily of things that are a familiar part of our routine, whether checking the mail, answering the phone or dealing with queries. But, in a similar way, do parents ever let go of their children, even when they are adults? Also, how is it that so many people find it hard to clear out their attics and cupboards and dispose of things they should have thrown away years ago, like letters and old schoolbooks? And why do some people hang onto bad relationships even when it is against all the advice of their family and friends?

Part of the human condition is that people don't let go easily of familiar routines in their lives and are more comfortable when they are in control of the detail. Anything that creates uncertainty increases people's anxiety and their resistance to letting go, reflected in the aphorism: 'people often prefer the certainty of misery to the misery of uncertainty'.

Tanzan and Ekido were once travelling together down a muddy road. A heavy rain was still falling. Coming around the bend they met a lovely girl in a silk kimono and sash, unable to cross the intersection.

> *'Come on girl'*, *said Tanzan at once. Lifting her into his arms he carried her over the mud.*
>
> *Ekido did not speak again until that night when they reached the lodging temple. Then he could no longer restrain himself.*
>
> *'We monks don't go near females'*, *he told Tanzan, 'especially not young and lovely ones. Why did you do that?'*
>
> *'I left the girl there', said Tanzan 'are you still carrying her?'* [1]

While the natural tendency is to hang on to what we know and are comfortable doing it is usually easier to let go to others if there are things you want to get done or achieve. One example is the Olympic athletes who in preparation for the games let go of many things, including their eating habits, social contacts, savings and even their jobs. How do they let go so easily? Clearly what helps is that they are totally focused on getting to the Olympics, doing a good time and winning a medal, and they let few distractions get in the way of that single-minded pursuit. Similarly, as a manager, it is much easier to handle the uncertainties of letting go to others if there are challenges on which to focus your time and energies. The place to start with delegation is not what you want to let go of, but what you want to hang on to for the future.

ENERGISE YOUR VISION

While managers spend a great deal of time on day-to-day routines, minor problems and queries, they are also responsible for changing things, making things happen and improving things for the future. Finding ways to commit to the longer-term challenges is not only an important first step in getting off the treadmill of daily activity but also the way to inspire your staff that their efforts are

Starting Delegation with Yourself

indeed leading to a better place. One potential source of future direction is having long-term ambitions or objectives, and a few basic questions may help explore where you want to go with them for the next year:

- What external challenges and threats are facing your area in the next year? e.g. new competitors, technology, legal constraints, labour shortages.
- What do you want to achieve or make happen in the next twelve months? e.g. change the reporting structure, certain work practices, reduce lead times, develop the team, introduce elements of multi-skilling, streamline the service or cut overheads.
- What challenges could inspire you and energise your staff over the next year? e.g. achieving ISO, reaching €2 million sales target, computerising the invoicing system.
- Do you identify with any of these as challenges for the next year?
  - Improving quality
  - Better teamwork
  - Reducing costs, rework or waste
  - Improving relationships with staff, customers, suppliers
  - Increasing market share
  - Recruiting new or better trained staff
  - Achieving a standard, e.g. ISO, Excellence Through People
  - Introducing new systems, structure, technology
  - Exploring new markets and new products
  - Retaining good staff

Although there is some advantage in having your ambitions in writing, they can also become a convenient way of hiding behind a lack of resolve to making them happen. Of more importance is committing time to reviewing your vision and values on a regular basis and fuelling them with shorter-term priorities and tasks.

21

> ### Clarifying the Vision
>
> Institutionalise your commitment to the future by scheduling half an hour in your Diary twice a year to plan for the next six months. One option is to write a one-page letter to yourself, reviewing your past achievements and identifying possible opportunities and challenges for the next half year. And, apart from the more tangible things like introducing a new product, reducing costs or improving delivery times, also include softer ideals like improving team spirit or creating a broader network of external contacts. Don't be too concerned that the letter sounds aspirational. It should reflect your values and dreams as well as tangible targets and objectives. Now underline the three or four key points in the letter by asking yourself what energises you most about the future and what is most likely to inspire your staff over the next year.
>
> An alternative exercise is to involve your team in the visioning exercise. Encourage each of them to write a one-page reflection on where they would like to see the unit in six months to a year's time that is a better place than now. Better still get them to draw a picture or diagram of their vision. Share those reflections at a meeting and agree three or four statements of intent – things that will move you in the direction of where you want to go. You could also spend some time considering what the group could do in the shorter-term (1–2 months) to get some immediate progress towards that vision.

Apart from setting your personal direction for the future, one of the main reasons for having a vision or strategic intent is to inspire others. At a time when many organisations are demanding significant improvements in output, service, quality and costs, an important part of any manager's job is to generate the commitment of their staff to what may be an uncertain journey into the future. And it does help

Starting Delegation with Yourself

if you make those aspirations into solid challenges on the basis that people respond more readily to goals and targets than to aspirations.

Dreams or aspirations are more accessible when they are expressed as goals, as with President Kennedy's pledge 'to land a man on the moon and return him safely to Earth by the end of the decade'. Although NASA officials had little idea at the time how it could be achieved they were energised by something that was clear and measurable. In putting the challenge to NASA Kennedy claimed some inspiration from a book by Irish writer Frank O'Connor which tells how as a young boy he and his friends would often make their way across open countryside. If they came upon a wall that seemed too high or too doubtful to climb they simply took off their hats and tossed them over, leaving them little option but to follow. Making the vision of space exploration into a solid goal also left NASA with little alternative but to pursue it as a clear challenge.

KEEP THE MAIN THINGS MAIN

While you may have an energising and inspiring vision for the future it is all too easy to lose sight of that challenge to the welter of day-to-day demands on your time. Anything long-term is inevitably at risk from the more immediate routines and urgency of the day. Keeping in touch with your long-term vision while operating in the short-term is made easier by identifying more immediate priorities for action that are within your line of sight (see Figure 2.1).

Converting longer-term challenges into shorter-term priorities for action can be as easy as drawing up a wish-list of all the things

Figure 2.1: Inspiring Vision to Actionable Tasks

```
                  Vision
Long-
term                               Abstract
                  Goals

                Priorities

Short-                             Concrete
term              Tasks
```

you would like to achieve over the next couple of months and selecting the two or three you have most energy for right now. The 'Golden Rule of Three', which applies to many situations, suggests that you can only focus on two or three things at any one time and trying to focus on too many things means you end up focusing on nothing. Restricting yourself to two or three priorities for the next few months does not mean that you lose sight of the other things on the wish-list – who knows, in a month's time you may have energy for others.

Setting Priorities for Action

Take five or ten minutes one day each month to brainstorm a list of all the things you want to achieve or get some mileage on in the next 2–3 months. In five minutes you are likely to come up with ten to fifteen items. Review the list and check that some of them relate to your longer-term goals. If not, then spend a few more minutes identifying things you could do in the next couple of months to further them. Next, select the three things for which you have most energy now, at least two of which should present a real challenge to the longer-term. And when selecting priorities for action don't pick things you wish for, but things you have real energy for now, either because you are concerned about them or you are excited about the possibility of success. (There are only two motivators in life – anxiety and excitement. Some things we do because we are 'anxious', such as study for exams, and others because we are 'excited', such as organising an overseas holiday.) Finally, identify how many hours you need to give each priority per week over the next few months to ensure success, and use your Diary to block out chunks of time to get those things done.

MANAGE THE PRIORITIES INTO ACTION

While coming down from longer-term ambitions to more solid priorities for action is relatively easy, managing them is more difficult because, by and large, people's energy is for what has to be done today and this week rather than for the next few months. Ask yourself this – when do people get energy for exams or holidays? Right – fairly close to the event. Since there is less energy in priorities than more immediate things it makes sense to break them into short-term tasks that can be done in the next few weeks and conveniently scheduled into your day.

As an example, take one of your priorities for the next few months and list all the things you could do in the next week or two to get the ball rolling. Think of the many small things that could be done almost immediately to get some mileage on them, such as drawing up a simple budget, writing a one-page proposal, arranging a short meeting with your boss, getting some information on the web or blocking out a couple of half hours in your diary for planning. And rather than trying to get any sequence into those tasks start on the easy ones first as a way of getting some early success and the energy to move on to other tasks.

Apart from breaking them into short-term tasks, managing the priorities also means making time for them. Some years ago Henry Mintzberg discovered, after trailing a group of executives around for a month, that rather than giving solid chunks of time to the important things in the job they spent less than ten per cent of their time on priorities, and most of their work was characterised by 'brevity, variety and discontinuity'.[2] While the fragmented and unfocused nature of the manager's day may be a legitimate response to the more immediate demands of customers and staff, there is evidence to suggest that much of it is because they end up doing work that their staff could be doing. The expression 'It's hard to remember you are there to drain the swamp when you're up to your ass in alligators' suggests how easy it is to end up as a busy alligator hunter when in fact you are employed as a swamp drainer. Letting go also means setting aside time in the day and week for the things you want to achieve as well as things you have to get done by blocking out time in your Diary or designating certain times in the week for those activities, e.g. two hours on Tuesday afternoons for the next month to get the staff training plan completed.

Finally, as an additional support to managing your priorities, have them in writing and strategically placed on the wall as a reminder of what you are trying to get done for the future – in the case of longer-term things, out of sight usually means out of mind. Get support from others, particularly your boss and staff by sharing the priorities, delegating some of the short-term tasks to key staff, reporting progress at staff meetings and getting others to nag you about your future commitments. With the best of intentions it is easy for the real challenges in the job to drift into the background unless you find ways of fuelling them with tasks and keeping them up front. And unless the real challenges in your job are kept to the fore it is unlikely that you are going to let go to your staff.

Starting Delegation with Yourself

RENEW YOUR LEADERSHIP STYLE

Apart from hanging on to the challenges in your own job, one of the main blocks to letting go to your staff could be your preferred style of managing. Although good leadership is often easier to recognise when it is absent than when it is present, most people know at least one manager who gets great performance and loyalty from their staff and who seems to be able to vary his or her style as the occasion demands. One of the more popular theories, called Situational Leadership, focuses on both the employee and the situation in determining an appropriate leadership response identifies four basic styles: Telling, Selling, Participating and Delegating.[3]

The Telling style is directive, involving the manager in giving detailed instructions on how the task should be done and with little focus on the needs of the individual. It is an appropriate style to use when staff are new to a task or there is a crisis. The Selling style is one where concern is shown for both the person and the task, involving the manager in providing clarity and encouragement. This style is more appropriate when managers are focusing on developing the ability and confidence of their staff. The Participating style involves the manager sharing ideas and concerns with their staff, giving them an opportunity to participate in how tasks should be completed and helping them resolve issues for themselves. This style is useful where the staff understand what they have to do but may be running into problems or need further support. Finally, the Delegating style is one where the manager is available but gives the individual or group almost complete control of a job and responsibility for resolving their own issues. As a style it is the ultimate aim for managers where employees are viewed as mature and responsible and as far as possible are left to get on with the job. While it doesn't imply an abdication of management it emphasises the manager in a supportive role, working with their staff and exercising a hands-off style.

Apart from identifying four styles of managing, the Situational Leadership Model also suggests that each of these styles is appropriate, depending on the level of readiness of the individual or group to take responsibility (their skills, experience, self-confidence and work attitudes). As they progress from being new and inexperienced in relation to the job or task, to where they are competent and confident, the model suggests that managers should move away from using 'hands-on' or controlling styles (Telling or Selling) to more 'hands-off' and empowering styles (Participating and Delegating) that emphasise treating the staff as mature in relation to the task or job. In summary, the model suggests that managers should, by developing and coaching their staff, move through the four styles to a position where individuals and the team are ready and willing to take full responsibility for what they are doing.

The process of moving through the style continuum is somewhat analogous to the child development model. Parents of very young children often use telling and selling styles as they encourage and coax them to learn basic life skills and avoid hazards. As they progress parents start to spend more time encouraging them to master essential skills such as reading, maths, making their beds and cleaning their room. Towards adolescence good parents, while being available, tend to back away from telling their children what to do or how to resolve their problems, in favour of helping them reach their own decisions and solutions. Ultimately good parents leave young adults to get on with their lives with minimal interference, while continuing to show an interest and in turn involving them in their own choices. But, while the leadership and child development models identify similarities they also highlight potential blocks in the staff development process.

In the same way that parents sometimes cocoon their children, blocking them from developing into mature adults, so managers often have a preferred style that has the same result. While it may be attractive for managers to use hands-on styles because they are comfortable and in control, it can also block individuals and groups from developing to their full potential. According to the theory, if

Starting Delegation with Yourself

you persist in using hands-on styles when your staff are able and willing to do the job, the most you can expect is they will move part of the way along the continuum towards maturity. As Roger Sant, ex-CEO of AES, reflects in an interview, 'It amazes me – in our society we tend to treat children like adults, and in the workplace we treat adults like children. Think about the responsibility we give to kids – the TV programmes and movies they watch or the subjects we expect them to know about and understand, like drugs and violence. But then, when they grow up, we put them in a work environment where every decision is made for them'.[4]

Not only are many managers intuitively attracted to hands-on styles, which may prevent their staff from maturing, but there is a self-fulfilling prophecy at work where people react negatively to close direction and control by acting in less than mature ways. It often serves to confirm a view in the mind of their managers that they are indeed irresponsible and not to be trusted, in turn leading to the exercise of even tighter control and staff becoming even more irresponsible.

As part of a study to examine the sociology of corrective institutions a team of social scientists at Stanford University led by Philip Zimbardo set up a mock prison in the basement of the Psychology department. It was comprised of three cells and a solitary confinement room that together were capable of holding twenty-one inmates. They advertised in the local papers for volunteer men and picked twenty-one who were adjudged to be the most normal and healthy. On the flip of a coin they assigned the volunteers as guards or prisoners. The guards were given uniforms and dark glasses and told their job was to keep order while the prisoners, in turn, were taken from their homes by the Palo Alto Police Department, blindfolded and brought to the prison where they were stripped, given prison uniforms with a number on both sides, and fingerprinted. So began a regular prison regime.

However, while the experiment was planned to last for two weeks it had to be abandoned after only six days as the researchers became increasingly alarmed at the growing hostility between the guards and prisoners. They were alerted to the behaviour of some guards, previously identified as pacifists, who within two days of entering the prison had started meting out cruel and unwarranted treatment, such as waking inmates in the middle of the night, making them do push-ups, stripping them and spraying them with fire extinguishers. They also observed the prisoners becoming overtly rebellious and increasingly preoccupied with revenge and plans for escape. In less than a week, and without prompting from the researchers, both groups had begun to adopt predictable roles, one as directive and controlling and the other as irresponsible and disaffected.

The Situational Leadership Model suggests that when individuals or groups run into performance or motivational problems the manager should move back to the previous style on the continuum (if using a Delegating style they should revert to a more Participating style). As an example, if the manager of a laboratory facility where the work group are responsible and well-motivated notices the performance of one individual has deteriorated over time, the model suggests they should help that person resolve the issue for themselves. In reality, faced with performance or motivational issues, many managers are inclined to move directly back to a more directive style, which almost inevitably exacerbates the problem and may lead to further de-motivation.

As a way of identifying your preferred style of managing people complete the questionnaire in Table 2.1. Better still, get some

Table 2.1: Your Preferred Style of Managing

Tick the appropriate space depending on whether you Agree (A), are Inclined to Agree (IA), are Inclined to Disagree (ID) or Disagree (D) with the statements below	A (1)	IA (2)	ID (3)	D (4)
1. I clearly tell my staff what I want from them and how the job should be done.				
2. I tend to keep pretty close to the work of my staff.				
3. I only make myself available to my staff if they need to clarify or discuss things.				
4. I tend to leave my staff alone to get on with their work although I am available if they need me.				
5. I ensure that my staff keep to the standards and procedures for doing the job.				
6. I tend to carefully monitor how things are going with my staff as a way of ensuring their performance and motivation.				
7. I only intervene in the work or relationships with my staff if their performance or behaviour is deteriorating.				
8. I like to show confidence in my staff by letting them make their own decisions and take risks.				

(Continued)

Table 2.1: *(Continued)*

Tick the appropriate space depending on whether you Agree (A), are Inclined to Agree (IA), are Inclined to Disagree (ID) or Disagree (D) with the statements below	A (1)	IA (2)	ID (3)	D (4)
9. I frequently check and review how my staff are doing on their various tasks and projects.				
10. I tend to give a lot of praise and encouragement and feedback to my staff on how they are doing.				
11. I see my job as mainly one of helping staff resolve things for themselves and meet their own needs in the job.				
12. I encourage my staff to set their own goals and priorities in the job.				

Assign a number to each answer as indicated and add up the scores as shown below. For which style do you have the highest score? While you could complete the checklist yourself, of more importance is how others perceive your style and the effect it may be having on them.

Questions 1 + 5 + 9 = Telling
Questions 2 + 6 + 10 = Selling
Questions 3 + 7 + 11 = Participating
Questions 4 + 8 + 12 = Delegating

Starting Delegation with Yourself

of your staff to complete the questionnaire in terms of how they view your style.

While managers may aspire to sharing responsibility, what makes for difficulties in practice is that staying in control of the detail is one of the ways in which they seek to reduce their anxiety about things being done right and on time. It tends to work against them, staff becoming irritated with their constant interference and as a result guarding themselves against criticism or badmouthing them to others. And the tendency for managers to over-control may be exacerbated by their own boss wanting them to stay in touch with the detail because it is also their preferred style. While there are situations in which hands-on styles are appropriate, human nature plays a significant part in attracting managers to styles where a self-fulfilling prophecy often confirms the view that people are basically irresponsible and need to be closely supervised.

One way of reversing the tendency to over-control is encouraging feedback on how your style may be affecting the performance of your staff. You could even regularise it as part of the performance review process. And, in seeking their views, use open questions that make it easier for them to respond, and for you to get detailed feedback you can action:

- In what areas of the job do you see yourself developing this year?
- Are there aspects of my work you could take on this year?
- How could we work better together?
- What could I do more of to support you in the job?
- What am I doing that you would like me to do more or less of?
- What blocks you from doing the job as you feel it should be done?
- What would you like from me that you are not getting?

An alternative approach to encouraging feedback from staff, if there are sufficient numbers, is to use a simple survey, such as in Table 2.2. One way to test the water is by asking one or two

Table 2.2: Staff Attitude Survey

Rate each item 1–9 according to the following scale
LOW 1   2   3   4   5   6   7   8   9 HIGH
needs – needs – adequate – does – does – superior to do   to do   well   really   performance much more   well more

To what extent do I:	Score 1–9
1. Give you challenging and rewarding work 2. Show concern for how you feel about and see the job 3. Make myself available to discuss your work 4. Show enthusiasm for what you are doing 5. Communicate clearly what I want from you 6. Give your ideas and suggestions a fair hearing 7. Give you support and encouragement along the way 8. Recognise and praise you for things done well 9. Help you to clarify priorities and goals in the job 10. Make time to listen to your concerns 11. Follow up regularly on how things are going 12. Celebrate your efforts and achievements in the job 13. Make time to explain what I want done 14. Seek your views on how things might be done better 15. Encourage and support you on projects and progress 16. Give you feedback in an encouraging and positive way	

Analysis: add the following sets of scores together to give a combined score under four headings:
Questions 1 + 5 + 9 + 13   = Clarifying expectations
Questions 2 + 6 + 10 + 14 = Getting acceptance
Questions 3 + 7 + 11 + 15 = Monitoring
Questions 4 + 8 + 12 + 16 = Rewarding

Starting Delegation with Yourself

individuals to complete the questionnaire and modify it on the basis of their responses. Carry out the briefing in a relaxed way while at the same time letting your staff know that you do want honesty and are willing to respond positively to the rating and their comments. And, if there are under performers or poor relationships in the group you could use the questionnaire to identify specific issues that may be contributing to the problem.

While delegation is essentially a process for letting go to others the place to start is with yourself. What ambitions and challenges do you want to focus on for the future? Where do you want your area to be in a year's time that is a better place than now? What are your priorities for the next few months and how much time do you need to give them each week to make significant progress? Also examine aspects of your management style that may be blocking you from letting go and sharing responsibility with others. It is often the way managers approach delegation that leads to a 'learned helplessness' in their staff, where as they become more controlling their people become less and less responsible. Letting go of real responsibility is a function of hanging on to what needs to be managed in your own job, which includes broad challenges for the future, shorter-term priorities for action, and using styles of managing that encourage others to share in the results you are trying to achieve.

CHAPTER 3

Challenging People to Perform

While the delegation process starts with focusing on the challenges in your own job and reviewing your management style it is also about learning to make demands on others to share your responsibilities. And while managers are sometimes reluctant to push their staff to take additional responsibility when they are already working under pressure it is important to constantly question their level of busyness. Everyone ends up being busy; the issue is 'busy doing what?' In the same way that managers may spend a great deal of time on the wrong things so it is important to challenge whether your staff are really assisting in what you are trying to achieve or are busy on routines which over time they have come to regard as their job.

Remind yourself that no one is there just to do things for today, even your staff. They also have a role in changing and improving things for the future, whether it is developing and broadening their own skills, or contributing to broader challenges for the department. While getting people to perform above the routine means helping them to manage their day-to-day busyness it is also about making demands on them to take increased responsibility and to translate those demands into action.

MAKE CLEAR DEMANDS ON YOUR STAFF

In communicating your expectations to others it is useful to examine how children get so much of what they want from adults. Children are usually much clearer than adults about what they want, which suggests that we actually unlearn how to be assertive. Most children are naturally assertive in three ways. Firstly, in making their demands clear and unambiguous. Rarely will you hear a child say 'I would like' or 'could you possibly' – instead they preface their demands with those two little words 'I want'. Unlike children, adults frequently couch their demands in language that is both vague and ambiguous, confusing what they really want with mixed messages that are rarely challenged. No wonder one research study concludes that over 70 per cent of workers are unclear about what their bosses want from them or how their performance will be measured.

Secondly, children make their demands specific, realising that if they are vague or ambiguous, as in asking for something to eat or a nice birthday present, they run the risk of getting something they don't want. So they ask for the large ice cream, an X Box 360 or a pair of Nike Sprint Sisters. And, in making their demands specific, children often quantify them in terms of the model or price and frequently attach a deadline, which is invariably NOW. In an informal but uncompromising way children convert their demands into clear goals for action.

Finally, and just as important, children learn that the first time you ask for something you don't stand a chance of being heard above the babble of more immediate issues, so they keep repeating what they want as a way of letting others know the importance they attach to that demand. In the lead up to birthdays or Christmas children start flagging their requests well ahead of time so there is plenty of opportunity to repeat them as the deadline approaches.

While adults are frequently aware of the tactics used by children in pursuing their demands, in essence they are the same skills that managers may have to re-learn as part of the process of getting things done through others. Getting staff on board with taking real responsibility requires managers to communicate their expectations in such a way that they understand what is required and know they will be supported and rewarded for their contribution to what the manager is trying achieve.

AGREE MUTUAL GOALS

Although there are a variety of ways of clarifying what you want from your staff, whether through frequent dialogue, role profiling, job descriptions, clear standards or agreeing limits of authority, one of the best ways of getting them to see beyond the routine is setting and managing their own goals.

Sometimes referred to as stretch goals, the clear implication is they should encourage individuals to set his or her sights on higher levels of achievement as a way of developing their skills and confidence. And many staff do need to be stretched and challenged as an antidote to finding a comfortable niche from where it is difficult to dislodge them when change or flexibility is required. While they may not welcome the process initially, as with going back to study or starting a new diet, most people want challenge in their lives and to see the benefits of their achievements in the form of recognition, reward and the development of new skills.

The 10 Per Cent Stretch

The next time you have a staff meeting try the following exercise as an energiser. Suggest to your staff that although the team may have been performing well they are capable of doing better. Ask them to stand up and work in pairs. With one person in each pair standing upright, their back to the wall and arms extended upwards, ask them to reach as high as they can. Get the other person to mark the spot reached by their fingertips either with a post it note or pencil. Now ask the person to really stretch themselves by extending their arms as far as they can go. Usually they reach quite a bit higher than the initial mark.

Use the exercise to encourage discussion on what a 10 per cent improvement in performance would mean for the unit, e.g. fewer delays, better service, improved delivery times, less complaints, increased bonuses and more compliments. Finally, involve them in brainstorming things the group could take on as stretch goals for the future.

While getting your staff to set goals is one of the best ways of challenging them to perform above the daily routine it should form part of an overall process that includes clarifying expectations, coaching sessions, periodic performance reviews and finding ways to recognise and reward them for their contribution. And whether it is part of an informal or formal performance management system the emphasis should be on dialogue and support rather than direction and control.

Should you decide to introduce some form of goal-setting in your area it is essential to bring concerns the staff may have out into the open at the start and show a willingness to discuss ways in which any mistrust could be reduced. Recently I was involved in introducing elements of a performance management system into a small organisation. When some staff opposition was expressed to the suggestion of having an individual bonus based on goal achievement a decision was made to keep the goals and bonus separate. Interestingly enough, after a couple of successful goal-setting and review sessions the staff themselves suggested the bonus in future should be directly related to individual performance.

> *Give me a stock clerk with a goal and I'll give you a man who will make history. Give me a man with no goals and I will give you a stock clerk* – J.C. Penney

Challenging People to Perform

If goal-setting has not been a part of your management style in the past you could start by arranging a one-on-one meeting with each member of your group as a way of encouraging two-way dialogue without formalising it as goal-setting and review. Check at the end of the meeting if they found the exchange useful and after a couple of meetings indicate that you want to start agreeing goals to be reviewed quarterly or bi-annually. Get them to start thinking about the challenges in their own jobs and give them a few examples of how a goal would look (see Table 3.1).

Before the next series of one-on-one meetings clarify in your own mind a couple of things you would like each individual to take on as challenges for the next 3–6 months, whether to meet a target or deadline, start a new project, change an aspect of their behaviour, take on an additional task, develop a new skill or share in one of your responsibilities. You might also get them to do some thinking prior to the meeting and submit possible goals in writing. As

Table 3.1: Possible Goal Areas

Goal Area	Examples
Routine	– Make the half-yearly budget by 1 July
	– Get 50 client files up to date by…
Innovation	– Develop a new information system by…
	– Complete a brochure for two new products by …
Reduction	– Reduce outstanding debts from 15 per cent to 12 per cent
	– Cut average overtime to three hours a week
Improvement	– Improve the telephone skills of two junior staff
	– Revamp the public office area
Personal	– Clarify supervisory role of a team leader
	– Pass two subjects in ECDL by…

part of the meeting get them to share what they see as their major challenges or priorities over the next 3–6 months and add your own. From the combined list agree three or four as mutual goals.

Also, take some time at the meeting to tighten up on their goals (make them specific, quantify them where possible and agree a deadline for completion). Finally, coach them on how to make a start on each goal. Encourage them to break what may seem to be daunting challenges into short-term tasks (simple things they could do in the next few weeks to get some early success and the energy to go on to the next stage). Not only does encouraging staff to break their goals into more manageable short-term tasks make it easier for them to access, but in terms of monitoring progress it is easier for you to follow up and feel reassured about how they intend to manage the next stage of the process (see Table 3.2).

Finally, discuss the help they may need in achieving their goals and suggest additional supports. Most real challenges require the practical support of others, whether you are trying to lose weight, decorate a room or gain a further qualification. Maybe they need to schedule some time with one of their colleagues to learn a bit more about a new system, attend an in-house training session or schedule a couple of hours with you. Possibly they also need to create a budget and get approval before moving forward on the project, or to offload some of their work to make time for the task. As much as possible encourage them to volunteer how they see themselves achieving the goals and the support they need as a way of keeping the ownership with them.

GROUP GOAL-SETTING AND REVIEW (GGSR)

Although goal-setting is traditionally carried out on a one-on-one basis it can also work well as a team exercise in two formats. Firstly, as a goal-sharing exercise there is some value in each individual member of the group identifying two to three goals for

Table 3.2: Example of Goals for the Next Six Months

Goals (Six months)	Short-Term Tasks (One month)
Complete the Marketing Plan by 30 June	– Draw up a schedule for completion and discuss with Jim – Carry out a survey of five main outlets – Arrange three meetings with the systems team – Get graphics done by CS
Get ten new prospects by 30 July	– Schedule five hours a week in the next month for telephoning prospects – Visit five companies – Review progress with TMcC weekly
Pass ECDL in PowerPoint and Excel by 30 July	– Book four coaching sessions with Lucy – Get training guide on graphics presentation – Spend two hours with Jim on Excel – Do a weekly progress report with graphics

themselves and stating them publicly in front of their colleagues. Apart from exposing them to what their colleagues are trying to achieve, the process of goal sharing allows peers to coach each other and offer mutual support. At the end of each quarter typically each individual is asked to make a short presentation on their progress and receive feedback and recognition from their colleagues. Not only can GGSR provide a rich learning experience for each individual in the team, as they see their peers identifying challenges and meeting them, but it also allows less ambitious staff to see what their colleagues are doing and to be inspired by their achievements.

A second form of group goal-setting and review (GGSR) involves everyone in the team, including the manager, identifying longer-term priorities for the department or section and identifying ways of sharing responsibility for achieving them as a group. The process is best started by involving the team in a brainstorming session designed to surface all the challenges and opportunities facing the area in the next six months, such as increased costs, high absenteeism, finding new markets for a product or improving after sales service. Without directing the exercise, ensure that your own concerns and challenges are also included on the list.

Making use of simple frameworks such as the SWOT (Strengths, Weaknesses, Opportunities, Threats) analysis may help the process of identifying goals, either through assigning each of the four boxes to smaller groups or with the whole group brainstorming the four boxes in turn. Having completed the SWOT brainstorm eliminate overlapping items to agree four or five as priorities for action over the next six months and allow some time to tighten them up as specific and measurable goals. Finally, invite each individual in the group to sign up to taking some responsibility for contributing to the achievement of one or several goals and identify a goal owner who will take overall charge of coordinating the effort. Encourage those who sign up to goals to schedule regular meetings and agree how they are going to manage themselves until the first review. At a quarterly review of group goals, each goal owner is usually required to make a presentation on their progress, what they intend to do next and any additional support required. Allow some time for their colleagues to challenge them and to offer constructive comment and feedback. As an exercise, not only does GGSR provide an opportunity for individuals to involve themselves in broader challenges for the department but it helps them learn about each other's jobs and how to work better as a team.

Challenging People to Perform

While the overall aim of goal-setting is to encourage individuals and teams to get in touch with challenges in their job or unit, equally it provides managers with a measure of performance on which to base their feedback. And, as a stimulus to improving performance, feedback on the challenges they set themselves is critical in getting staff to see beyond a narrow definition of the job. In the absence of feedback on results, goal-setting is a bit like playing golf in the dark or ten-pin bowling without the pins, enjoyable for a while but hardly energising or stretching in the longer-term.

Giving your staff feedback on their goals can take place at several levels. Firstly, it can be integrated into the normal routine of checking progress or recognising effort – 'I see you met with Jim', 'well done on getting a first draft in on time' or 'how much headway have you made on the competitor survey?' Alternatively, some time could be scheduled into the week for managing by wandering around (MBWA) to follow up on the efforts of individual staff, particularly where you feel they need encouragement or may be discouraged by their lack of progress.

Secondly, feedback can be integrated into the normal work review process, whether as part of the Management Information System (MIS) or by reporting progress at regular meetings. If a major goal for your section is to reduce waste, rework, errors, returns, labour turnover or absenteeism, one of the best ways of focusing attention on those challenges is to start measuring them, making the results public and reviewing them at weekly meetings.

Thirdly, feedback on goals can form part of a more formal review process at the end of each period. According to Lee Iacocca, one-time President of Chrysler, the quarterly review system sounds almost too simple, but it works. In support of regular goal-setting and review he offers five positive arguments:[1]

1. It allows the person to be their own boss and to set their own goals
2. It makes individuals more productive and self-motivated
3. It provides an opportunity for ideas and concerns to be surfaced
4. It prevents the good guys from being overlooked and the bad guys from hiding
5. It forces dialogue between a manager and his or her staff

Emphasising the importance of dialogue as key to the success of any job review process, Iacocca reflects that in an ideal world you wouldn't need structures to ensure that dialogue takes place between a manager and his/her staff. But, particularly if they don't get on too well with some of their staff, having to sit down and decide on mutually agreed goals and reviewing them once a quarter is almost bound to improve the working relationship.

> *The combined effect of goal-setting and feedback was well illustrated by a research project designed to identify ways of encouraging householders in New Jersey to reduce their electricity consumption. One group of homeowners was challenged to reduce their usage by a significant 20 per cent, while another was asked to reduce it by a modest 2 per cent. Half the households in each group were given feedback on a daily basis by researchers updating a tracking sheet on the outside of their patio windows while the other half were not given any feedback at all. In addition a third group of householders who were outside the*

goal-setting process were given daily feedback on their consumption and simply asked to do their best. While the findings clearly showed that the group with the challenging goal and feedback did best, equally interesting was that the group with no goal but who were given feedback did better than those with an easy goal and no feedback. The study concluded that setting stretch goals is better than having easy goals, but to be really effective goals they must be accompanied by regular feedback.[2]

CLARIFY ROLES AND ACTIVITIES

Although there has been a long history of research on goal-setting since the seminal work of Latham and Locke[3] showed a clear relationship between setting challenging goals and achieving results, the recent interest in performance management reflects a growing need in many organisations to push increased and broader responsibility down to lower levels. However, for many situations goal-setting is not the most appropriate mechanism for clarifying expectations with staff. And there are obvious downsides to goal-setting, especially when it is linked to pay or bonuses, which can lead staff to focus on their goals at the expense of other aspects of the job. In addition, goals are usually expressed in output terms such as meeting specific targets or deadlines, which tends to discount the inputs required to achieve them, such as improving customer relationships, learning new systems or developing teamwork. As such, goal-setting is probably more suited to manufacturing and technical service situations where it is easier to measure and quantify the outputs, but less suitable for broader jobs like research or the caring services where the outputs are less measurable and quality is critical.

Where goal-setting is not the preferred option for clarifying expectations with your staff other possibilities include Role

Clarification and Job Descriptions. Although discussed in more detail in Chapter 8, Role Clarification consists of a periodic review of each individual's function, on the basis that how people view the job determines where they put their time and energy. And, as with managers, it is easy for staff to end up energetically pursuing activities that bear little relation to why they were employed. While Role Clarification can be a formal exercise it is essentially an opportunity to engage in a two-way dialogue on the essence of the job: why does it exist, what is the purpose of the job and what is the boss demanding of the jobholder? On the basis that roles change over time, in the same way that the parenting role changes as children develop and the roles of policemen and teachers have to adjust to changes in society or new legislation, so it is useful now and again to remind your staff of their contribution to the work of the department (which also suggests that reviewing the function of the department is a useful starting place for role clarification).

While a periodic review of the role and functions of your staff can be useful, particularly during restructuring or rapid change, one of the more traditional ways of clarifying expectations is through Job Descriptions, a review of the tasks to be carried out by the jobholder. Although Job Descriptions have fallen into some disfavour in recent years, on the basis that they tend to straitjacket the jobholder, they can be useful for clarifying what your staff are expected to do and where they should be putting their time.

Job Description Review

A simple exercise for encouraging your staff to get in touch with the realities of their job is to ask them to draw up a simple shopping list of activities on which they spend their time. This could be done individually or as a group. Alternatively, encourage them to compile the list over a couple of days, adding new tasks as they arise. When you are fairly sure the list is complete get them to estimate the average hours, to the nearest fifteen minutes, they spend on each activity per week. Add up the estimate and check the total against their average working week. A margin of three or four hours is acceptable.

Now, get them to analyse the data as follows.

1. Identify the four to six key tasks on the list – not the tasks they have to do or those which take most time, but the important tasks. Put a P (for Priority) beside those activities. Add up the hours spent on P's and calculate the percentage over the total hours worked on that day.
2. Tick the activities they could delegate (including the P's). Remind them there are four ways to delegate work including saying 'no', spending less time on some things and pushing some things back to other people. Add up the hours on D's (Delegatable tasks) and calculate the percentage over the total hours worked that day. (While it may be that they can't let go of the whole task perhaps they could delegate part of it.)
3. Finally, get them to identify three activities to which they would like to give more and less of their time in future – they may not be on the list or may currently be part of your job.

Having completed the analysis give them ten minutes to write a one-page letter either to you or to themselves, reflecting on the analysis and what it is telling them about the way they are currently using their time. Encourage them to identify ways they could make the job more challenging for themselves and assist you better for the future. After adding your own comments draft it up as their Job Description to be reviewed at a specific date in the future.

Of importance when reviewing Job Descriptions, as with Role Clarification, is that they form part of an overall process for clarifying expectations and are not seen as an end in themselves. Some would even argue that Job Descriptions should only be created when there is a need to have them, such as during a reorganisation or when individuals are new to a job. In order for them to be seen as a useful tool in clarifying the demands of a job they should involve the person and their manager drawing up a list of the activities that take up the person's time and agreeing it as a basic document for refinement. After identifying all the possible tasks or activities the list should be reduced to just the main activities rather than the pages of detail seen in some job descriptions. It also makes sense as part of the process to identify the five or six priority activities in the job and to flesh those out in more detail.

In refining job descriptions it may also be helpful to group activities or tasks under separate sub-headings, such as things that are done routinely and occasionally, those done on a daily, weekly and annual basis, or the technical, clerical and personnel aspects of the job. Alternatively, arrange the activities according to their descending order of importance in the job and agree how that order might change over the next year.

Letting go to staff means making demands on them to share in your responsibilities, encouraging them to broaden their skills and getting them to see beyond their daily routine to the real challenges in the job. And while they may not actively look for increased responsibility most people welcome the energy and recognition that challenge and achievement provide. In his best-selling book *Psycho-Cybernetics*, Dr Maxwell Maltz concludes from his years as a plastic surgeon that satisfaction and self-esteem come from what we do rather than how we see ourselves.[4] Having treated many patients who believed that a change in their appearance would lead to an improvement in their self-image he discovered that while it was true for some people, many others felt no different after the surgery than they did before. Suggesting that self-esteem comes mainly from what we achieve in our lives, whether raising children, excelling at sports or being successful in a career, Maltz concludes:

> *We are engineered as goal seeking mechanisms... We are built to conquer the environment, solve problems, achieve goals, and find no real satisfaction or happiness in life without obstacles to conquer and goals to achieve.*

Although it may appear some staff would prefer the certainty of a routine job to the challenge of taking on new levels of responsibility it is just as likely they have settled for that over time. And whether it is a valid assumption or not, in an ever-changing and demanding environment organisations can no longer afford to have people settling into comfortable positions and doing what they have always done. For most organisations to survive and grow in today's environment it is important to have switched-on staff who have the capacity and flexibility to respond to changing circumstances and, as such, it is the job of the manager to get the best out of their people and help them get more out of themselves. Good staff will only be attracted, motivated and retained if they are encouraged to share in the future aspirations of the area in which they are working, are constantly mastering new skills and have clear challenges to succeed. Managers are there to provide the conditions in which those things can happen.

CHAPTER 4

Coaching for Confidence

Without doubt, the best boss I ever had was in my early career when I was cutting my teeth as a manager. Apart from placing a great deal of trust in my ability to do the job, inexperienced as I was, he also gave me time. One of my clear memories is of him putting his head round the door to ask if I was free for coffee. On those occasions we sat and chatted, mainly about my work, and I also learned about the challenges and frustrations he was facing in the job. Whenever I think of coaching or the qualities of a good coach I think of him.

While the immense growth in communications technology has lead to an increasing use of e-mail, the web and intranets to share information with staff the best form of communication still remains what is called 'frequent – face-to-face – dialogue'. Frequent contacts between staff and their manager means there is ongoing opportunity to repeat what he or she wants and for staff to respond – as a result there are few surprises. Face-to-face contact is also critical in building relationships with staff since it has more impact than impersonal memos or e-mails, and because much of the way we relate to others is non-verbally. Research suggests that 93 per cent of the effect in communications is not from the words but in how they are said, 38 per cent from tone of voice and 55 per cent from visual clues such as posture, eye movements and gestures. The significance of both the words and the music (the non-verbals) is that when they are in alignment people are more likely to trust what is being said by the other person than when there is an absence of non-verbal cues.

Finally, and equally important in building relationships, is that a dialogue takes place in which each person seeks to understand how the other sees and feels about whatever is under discussion. In essence, good coaching is about making time for frequent – face-to-face – dialogue with your staff, whether formally at job reviews or more casually over coffee. And the overall objective of most coaching situations is to develop the confidence and competence of each staff member to take more ownership and responsibility for what they are being asked to do.

Reasons for coaching staff:

- To monitor how things are going
- To clarify their roles, tasks and activities
- To encourage staff to take more responsibility
- To deal with performance or behavioural issues
- To keep problems (monkeys) with staff
- To confront difficult staff

Many managers have seen the illustration in Figure 4.1 and been asked to guess the age of the woman – if you haven't, roughly what age is she? While some people find it easy to see the outline of an old woman and others a younger woman, more interesting is that having seen it one way it is often difficult to see the other person. Only by examining it several times is it possible for many to see there are indeed two women in the picture.

One of the key messages from the graphic is that when people see things differently, instead of trying to see them from the other person's view they are more likely to insist on their own view being right. As George Bernard Shaw once suggested, conflict is never between two people, one of whom is right and the

Figure 4.1

other wrong – it is always between two people who are both right. Frequently it is more fruitful in communicating or influencing others to acknowledge their view as legitimate and worth hearing. In the same way that good relationships are built on sharing the complete picture so the key to building trust and avoiding misunderstanding lies in two important skills: listening and feedback.

INFLUENCE STAFF THROUGH ACTIVE LISTENING

Generally acknowledged as the father of modern communications, psychologist and therapist Carl Rogers suggests that it takes courage to really listen to another person's point of view, particularly if their opinions are very different from your own, as it may result in having to change your view. And for most people, according to Rogers, the threat of being changed is a frightening prospect.[1] However, to develop good working relationships and avoid the misunderstandings that lead to mistrust you have to do just that. And while the objective in listening may be to understand the other person's point of view, it is also about helping the other person think through and confront problems and issues for themselves.

> *One clear example of the power of listening is the work of the Samaritans, an agency dedicated to helping people who are anxious, depressed or suicidal. In their literature they always promote themselves as a listening agency, saying, 'we never give advice'. They know that if someone is agitated or distressed it isn't helpful to tell them to look on the bright side, find ways to keep themselves busy or get a hobby to take their mind off their problems. When people are confused or anxious it is more productive to help them listen to themselves as a way of encouraging them to take ownership of whatever actions they are willing to take.*

Not only is listening to your staff helpful in getting them to think through how they see and feel about what they are doing, it is often the best way to coach them on improving their performance and encouraging them to take on new challenges. And while there are a number of specific skills in active listening the three most important are:

1. Showing a willingness to listen
2. Encouraging them to talk
3. Summarising back what you hear

Show a Willingness to Listen

While having a genuine interest in others may be considered a trait more than a skill, it is a competency that many managers need to develop. Whether or not you are a good listener in the work situation you probably are willing to listen when it comes to your own children or close friends. But when managers are busy or don't get on with certain individuals or groups it is easy to be seen as a bad listener, so it may be important to make time for one-on-ones, touching base with staff or having regular briefing sessions with your team.

And if you decide to schedule time for one-on-ones or team meetings start by declaring an interest in what your staff have to say and encourage them to be open and honest in their opinions. As Elaina Zuker comments in *The Seven Secrets of Influence*, good listening does not mean accepting everything that people say, but it does demand that you evaluate what the person is saying after you have the information rather than filtering what they say so you never actually hear their views.[2]

Encourage Them to Express Views and Feelings

As a rule, when leading questions are introduced into a conversation, such as 'you must find the job interesting?' or 'surely things are easier now?', it invites misleading information or agreement with the view implied in the question. Similarly, closed questions such as 'have you finished the update yet?' or 'do you like this job?' at best gives limited information and could possibly be misleading if the answer is a casual 'yes, almost' or 'well, it's not so bad'.

To find out how your staff see and feel about an issue, or the job in general, it is best to incline towards open questions such as:

- How are things going at the moment?
- Where are you with the project?

- When do you see things improving?
- What is getting in the way of meeting the deadline?
- Where could you make a start?
- How are the team responding to the new system?
- What resources do you need to get the job done?
- Who else needs to be involved in the meeting?

Apart from what, where, when, how, who and why questions, also include open invitations to talk and precision questions designed to get more specific detail from the other person

- Open invitations
  - Tell me a little about the job?
  - Give me a few examples?
  - Can you elaborate on that?
- Precision questions
  - What do you mean by simple?
  - Where precisely are his needs?
  - What exactly do you require?

Summarise the Words and Feelings

One of the most difficult interpersonal skills to master, and yet critical to good listening, is summarising what the other person is saying. Paraphrasing what the other person says (sometimes called mirroring) is important both as a way of letting them know you are listening and for reflecting back what they have just said. In the same way that glancing in a mirror is often enough to suggest that people change their glasses or get a haircut, so short summaries often lead people to change or add to what they have already said, for example:

A – 'I don't think we have built in enough time for possible delays on the project.'
B – 'You think it may overrun?'

A – 'Well, not if we put resources into reducing the bottlenecks and rework.'
B – 'We need additional help.'

Or:

A – 'So you feel the service from IT has got worse in the last six months?'
B – 'Yes it has, but they also have critical problems with staffing that we need to sit down and discuss.'
A – 'We need a meeting.'
B – 'Well, a meeting would be one way, but I am not sure it is the most immediate option.'
A – 'Other approaches may be better in the short-term.'

On the basis that a great deal of the way we communicate is non-verbally, in addition to summarising the content of what the other person is saying, it is often useful to reflect the feelings you sense in their tone of voice, posture or gestures. And summaries are also a good way of slowing down a conversation and keeping control if the other person is inclined to ramble or become emotional. For example:

- You are angry at the way you have been treated.
- I sense a real frustration in your voice.
- You seem to be less excited about the project than I am.
- It is a complex and confusing issue.

Although some managers are intuitive listeners, for others it is an important skill they may need to develop. While one way to hone your listening skills is attending a communications course, another is to start practising the elements of active listening in your everyday dealings with your staff. Rogers suggests that the next time you get into an argument or disagreement with an individual or group you should institute a rule that each person can only speak after they have accurately summarised what the other person has said. Probably a more practical approach is when you are having coffee with one of your staff and they are talking about an issue, commit yourself for just three minutes to trying to understand their point of view by doing nothing else but asking open questions and summarising back what you hear. See the effect it has, and don't judge your efforts too harshly.

> *John was attending a training course on communications where on the first day he learned the basic mechanics of good listening. As usual when he arrived home that evening he decided to find out how his son had got on at school and to try out the skills he had learned. He came in the following day with an obvious energy to learn more. 'Normally', he said, 'when I go home in the evenings I say to my son, "have you done your homework yet?" or "were things alright at school today?", to which I get the briefest of replies. Yesterday evening', he said, 'I asked him "How did you get on at school today?" and "what did you cover in Mr Peter's class?" I also tried to summarise back what he was saying: "so it was a good day", and, "you really enjoyed the geography class". The end result was I had a fifteen-minute chat with my son and that hasn't happened for months.'*

Although showing a willingness to listen, asking questions and summarising are key skills in any coaching situation, other techniques that also encourage staff to share their views include using minimal reinforcement as a way of encouraging the person to keep talking, such as 'uh-huh's, or 'yes go on', pausing when it is appropriate to let them think, and keeping good eye contact. While it is human nature that we are generally more comfortable giving advice or expressing our own views it is often much more useful to listen and help staff listen to themselves. It is at the core of good coaching.

BENEFIT FROM THE FEEDBACK EFFECT

The second key skill in coaching is feedback. Not only is giving and seeking feedback critical to building good relationships, it is also something staff expect from their managers in the same way that children want constructive comments from parents on their academic achievements and sporting successes, and spouses give to each other as a way of deepening the relationship.

[Dilbert comic strip: Panel 1 — Manager: "FROM NOW ON I'LL BE MANAGING BY EXCEPTION." Panel 2 — "IF I DON'T TALK TO YOU FOR MONTHS, ASSUME YOU'RE DOING A GOOD JOB." Panel 3 — "...OR THAT YOUR PROJECT ISN'T IMPORTANT...OR I DON'T REMEMBER YOUR NAME."]

However, while it is a powerful tool in building relationships, managers are often reluctant to give feedback to their staff for fear that it may de-motivate them or lead to negative reaction. Having worked with many organisations on improving their job review processes it is usual after the first series of reviews to invite the staff who have been reviewed to complete a short evaluation that is given anonymously to their manager. In many cases it highlights a clear discrepancy between their boss's willingness to listen and his or her reluctance to give them specific feedback from which they could learn.

> *In a simulation on creative problem-solving a group of MBA students were told that their performance would be compared with others who had done a similar exercise. While some of the students were praised by the researchers others were criticised and yet others were given no feedback at all. In a later evaluation it was found that those who heard nothing from the researchers suffered as great a blow to their self-confidence as did those who were criticised.*[3]

What then is good feedback? Generally it comes in two varieties: corrective and encouraging. Corrective feedback is aimed at getting the person to modify aspects of their behaviour or performance, while encouraging feedback is designed to get them to continue improving at something they are doing well or approximately right. And a comment attributed to Barbara Cartland illustrates the wisdom of catching people doing things approximately right, 'A wise woman', she said 'will always tell a man he is a wonderful lover and hope that one day he will become one'.

But while giving feedback to staff has great potential for improving their performance or behaviour, to be useful it must be accepted. Although there may be things you want to get across, unless there is a genuine resolve to act on the feedback it is neither productive nor useful. In making job-related feedback more acceptable a few practical rules help to ensure that it does not undermine the person's self-confidence.

It Should Be Descriptive Rather Than Evaluative

No matter how difficult or incompetent they may be, anything that undermines a person's self-esteem will tend to be rejected – try telling someone they are stupid or thoughtless without getting a negative reaction. Generally it is best to give people the facts and let them reach their own conclusions: 'you have missed the last three deadlines' or 'the CEO was really impressed by your proposal'. Alternatively, or in addition, describe the effect of their behaviour on yourself and on others: 'I was embarrassed at the meeting by not having your figures' or 'your enthusiasm for the project lifted the whole team'.

It Should Be Specific Rather Than Vague

While it is less easy to influence people with vague or general feedback it is also more likely to be challenged. Telling someone that their report was excellent may be a nice compliment but it doesn't tell them how to improve their reports for the future, in the same way that telling one of your staff their performance isn't up to standard is less than helpful. Conversely, telling someone after a presentation that their PowerPoint slides were simple and really focused people's attention, or that there were three complaints from clients about cancelled meetings in the last month, leaves the receiver with clear options and less ability to challenge the facts.

It Should Be Timely

In the normal course of events feedback should energise staff to respond in a positive way. Feedback that is offered some months after an event has probably lost a great deal of its potency, while if the feedback on a highly charged issue is given too close to the event the emotions may prevent the receiver from hearing the message. If there is a high degree of emotion on either side it is usually best to allow a cooling off period before confronting the issue.

It Should Be Sparing

It is often difficult for people to acknowledge corrective feedback, so it is usually best to do it in private, keep it short and let them know that in all other respects you are happy with their performance. And if you are giving feedback at a job review try to avoid overloading them simply because you have the opportunity: 'while you are here I may as well mention a couple of other things'. Generally it is better to identify one or two key issues, explore them with facts and examples and agree ways to work on them together.

> *In a project aimed at reducing high levels of absenteeism the employees at Parkdale Mills were set a goal to achieve 93 per cent attendance for a period of three weeks. Every employee's name was put on a chart and each day they received a blue dot if they were present and a red dot if absent. Their performance against the overall goal of 93 per cent attendance was indicated weekly on a chart that showed the percentage of employees present each day. Each person attending was complimented daily by the shift supervisor and those who were absent were welcomed back the next day without reprimand. Instead the supervisor reminded the employee of the attendance chart and simply asked for their help in achieving the goal. Almost directly after the feedback process was implemented average attendance improved and for the following nine weeks the attendance averaged*

94.3 per cent, and on one week reached 100 per cent. Equally important, teamwork and enthusiasm that were previously lacking improved greatly.

DEAL WITH DEFENSIVE BEHAVIOUR

However, no matter how delicately you plan to present feedback there is always a possibility it will result in defensiveness, either because you have violated the rules or you are dealing with people who are particularly sensitive or low in self-esteem. And the potential for upsetting people and dis-improving the situation is sometimes enough to stop managers giving feedback at all, hoping that the individual will get the message in some other way, or punishing them for something they don't even know they are doing.

In dealing with defensive behaviour it is important to recognise that it is a natural reaction to any threat, real or imagined; a primitive response that is exhibited by some people in overt ways and others in less obvious and more acceptable ways. Some of the more typical forms of defensive reactions include anger, longwinded explanations (explaining away the feedback), head nodding (apparent agreement), reversal (blaming you or others for their poor performance), flight into health (assuring you that it won't happen again), withdrawal (avoiding contact) and bad mouthing (blaming you behind your back).

The key issue in handling reaction is not the defensiveness itself, but the fact that it gets in the way of the person hearing and acting on the feedback. If one of your staff appears to be rejecting your feedback, either overtly or in their body language, there are four basic ways of responding:

Go Back to Listening

If an individual is angry, irritated or apparently explaining away your feedback the easiest route is to go back to asking open questions like, 'well, how do you see the situation?' or 'what's your own view?' Alternatively you can reflect the emotion in their defensiveness: 'you seem to be angry with my comments' or 'I see you are nodding your head, but I get the feeling you are not in agreement'. Inviting the other person to talk about their defensiveness often leads to them accepting, at least in part, your feedback.

Be Firm

Where a clear standard has been broken, one option is to acknowledge their side of things but keep returning to the rule or demand. If, for example, there is a clear regulation on working hours, keep repeating the message: 'I appreciate your difficulties with transport but we start at 9.00 a.m.', or 'I know they sometimes get in the way of the job but wearing safety goggles is not optional'. If, on the other hand, something is not a formal rule but you are entitled to demand it from your staff it is useful to keep coming back to the demand, for example, 'getting the reports in on Thursday is a priority for me – I need your figures by Wednesday' or 'I know he can be difficult but there is no justification for having arguments in front of customers'.

Label Your Own Feelings

Often, when confronted by their boss, individuals are more focused on their emotions than on their behaviour or performance. In those situations it can help to let them know that you are also affected by the situation through labelling your own feelings: 'you are angry Jim, but let me tell you I am also angry', or 'I too am frustrated because I know you are capable of better'. Not only does labelling your feelings help communicate them to the other person but it also allows you to discharge your emotions without showing obvious anger or frustration.

Stay in Your Adult

One useful tool in dealing with defensive behaviour is Transactional Analysis, which suggests that people communicate from three ego states: parent, adult and child. Usually we operate from our adult state, but in times of stress sometimes revert to the others, which can have positive as well as negative effects. When someone becomes defensive they are often acting out of their parent state (laying down the law) or their child state (temper tantrum). Typically when that happens the other person responds similarly, by raising their voice or blaming the other, which results in a further escalation. The practical benefits of transactional analysis is it recognises when the other person is acting out of their negative parent or child the best response is to remain in your adult state rather than raising your voice or laying down the law. Invariably they will return to responding in adult ways themselves.

As with other aspects of interpersonal skills the principles of giving feedback and dealing with defensiveness are almost self-evident. But when you are dealing with your own emotions or have some anxiety about the possibility of reaction it becomes a much more difficult task. Nevertheless, even if you have to deal with negative reaction it is important to give feedback to your staff in as honest a way as possible, partly to improve their performance or behaviour but also to encourage more openness and trust in the relationship. And as Jack Welch of GE argues in his autobiography, 'it is unfair for managers to be less than honest with their staff – if individuals don't know they have performance deficiencies how can they be expected to improve? Should they find out later in their careers that you deliberately kept feedback from them they will feel cheated that you denied them an opportunity to reform or get another job where they may have succeeded'.[4]

Hanging On and Letting Go: The Art of Real Delegation

PUSH BACK THE MONKEYS

One of the most common myths in management is that delegation is essentially a top-down process. In reality most delegation is upwards, of issues, problems and queries coming from staff. Not only do many managers fall into the trap of doing things themselves because their staff are evidently busy, but they also become victims to the volume of queries and problems they get from their staff. The result is a double whammy, where they end up not having sufficient time for their own priorities and their willingness to give expert advice leads to their staff coming with even more queries.

Feeding the Monkeys

In a seminal *Harvard Business Review* article, Oncken and Wass illustrate how easily managers take 'monkeys' from their staff and make them their own.[5] Casual interactions in the corridor where staff open with comments like, 'we've got a problem' or 'what do you want me to do about X?', often lead the manager to respond with 'leave it with me' or 'let me think about it and I'll get back to you'. The authors argue that if managers are to get sufficient time for their own priorities they have to reduce the amount of staff-imposed time by managing the monkeys and using that newfound discretionary time for coaching and motivating their staff.

If you give your staff solutions to their problems:

- They will come with even more problems
- They will learn nothing – giving advice is not coaching
- They have little ownership for implementation – if it is wrong it was your solution

The key to coaching staff when they come with problems is, as much as possible, to keep ownership with them. One of the ways in which managers unwittingly take ownership is by collecting information: 'how many are yet to be completed?' or 'what is the current situation with the customer?' Asking questions tends to create an expectation in the mind of the individual that the manager will come up with a solution in the same way that patients who share their symptoms with a doctor expect them to take responsibility for making them better. However, as patients may listen but ignore their doctor's advice (according to the British Medical Association, 30 per cent of people never complete the recommended course of treatment) so staff have less ownership for solutions that are presented to them, learning little except the next time they have a similar problem to go straight back to their manager.

Being available to your staff while at the same time helping them take more ownership of their monkeys may mean establishing a rule that if they have a problem they come with a suggested solution or at least some options. It may also, on occasions, mean giving them a hearing but sending them away to decide for themselves or to come back with a proposal. In other circumstances it can also mean pushing the problem straight back with questions like:

- What are the options on this?
- What have you done so far to resolve the issue?
- Who could help on this?
- What might be a first step?
- What do you want to do about it?
- Where do you go from here?

> *Once again Margaret had been interrupted by Jim arriving with a problem he should be handling himself. And once again she had responded to his cheery 'have you got a minute' with a fifteen-minute discussion and agreeing to telephone the customer. She had to try something else.*

> *The following Tuesday when Jim arrived unannounced with another query, Margaret resolved to handle things differently.*
>
> *'I haven't been able to finalise the Cummins job – what do you want me to do?' asked Jim.*
>
> *Margaret took a deep breath and replied, 'well, what do you think you should do?'*
>
> *She followed up with questions like 'who could help with this?' and 'how much could you get done before lunchtime tomorrow?' She also reflected back what she heard: 'so the problem can be fixed' and 'the Thursday deadline gives you three full days'. Although it had taken a few minutes of her time she felt relieved that she hadn't taken on Jim's problem. As she continued to push things back to Jim, while coaching him on how to resolve similar issues for himself, at his next review she was able to praise him for how well he had been doing. They also agreed some guidelines on issues where she needed to be involved, and sensed from the non-verbals that Jim had grown in confidence over the past few months.*

Human nature is such that we generally feel more comfortable telling staff what to do or giving them advice rather than coaching. Maybe at times individuals do need direction, such as when they are new to the job or task, or where a rapid response is required. But, as the saying goes, 'help isn't always helpful'. Ask yourself whether giving advice satisfies your need to feel helpful or their need to be helped. And if the aim is to get your staff to take more responsibility for resolving their own issues then keeping ownership with them is more important than coming up with a quick solution. 'Monkeys' are an opportunity for coaching staff but one that managers often fail to take.

Rules for Keeping Monkeys with Staff

- Treat problems as opportunities to coach your staff
- Keep ownership by helping them examine the options and identify first steps
- Have a norm that you will only entertain problems if they also come with options or a proposal
- Assist your staff by directing them to where they can get help
- Push problems back with confronting questions like 'what have you done so far?' or 'what would you suggest?'

While coaching is a key skill in delegation it is also one that can be learned through finding opportunities to practice the basic techniques of listening and giving feedback. But coaching is also about giving time to your staff, even if they are busy and think they don't need guidance or help. Making coaching a part of your delegation style also means scheduling time for one-on-ones with staff, having regular quarterly reviews and blocking out time for MBWA in your Diary.

While there are many other ways to bring out the best in people the evidence of good mentors and best bosses points to the importance of coaching as critical to staff developing the confidence to take on increased responsibility. And coaching is not telling – it is about helping staff to take ownership for what they are doing while avoiding the tendency to take back responsibility by resolving problems for them. Unless you act otherwise they will persist in coming with queries and you will find yourself too busy to take on the real challenges in your own job or sufficient quality time to coach them.

CHAPTER 5

Motivating Staff Beyond Expectations

One of the questions I frequently ask managers on training programmes is 'are people naturally lazy?' The responses generally range from 'yes' and 'no' to 'sometimes' and 'it depends'. After some discussion, which includes examples of how people can be lazy at work and yet very active in their personal lives, and the appetite that young children have for learning, most are part-way to being convinced that people are naturally active but something happens in the work situation to make them lazy.

Apart from the obvious examples of children at play and adults engaging in sporting activities, there is a substantial body of evidence that people also want to be actively involved at work. If you look back to the first day in any new job, most people are excited about the thought of meeting colleagues for the first time, the opportunities for developing new skills and the chance to make a contribution. And yet many of those same people, in a few short months, are showing classic symptoms of disinterest and low energy. How is it that some people go from being excited and switched on about what they are doing to being complacent and disinterested in only a few short months, and how can managers prevent it from happening?

While ensuring their staff do not become complacent is a major task for managers an even greater challenge is getting them on board with the changing needs of the business and keeping them flexible to the demands of customers and the competition. How to energise your staff beyond the more immediate demands of the day and encourage them to consistently give of their best is one of the key skills in managing people.

SYMPTOMS AND CAUSES OF DE-MOTIVATION

What managers first recognise as low motivation are visible symptoms in the form of grievances, inflexibility, absenteeism, inconsistency or irresponsibility (see Table 5.1). Faced with such symptoms organisations are inclined to look for better ways to control them through a variety of initiatives such as attendance bonuses, publicising statistics or tightening the disciplinary process. Likewise, managers also tend to react to what they see as creeping irresponsibility in their staff by becoming less trusting and more hands-on and controlling. Not only does the reaction frequently add to the malaise they are trying to remedy but their attempts at treating the symptoms often have the same outcome as

Table 5.1: Symptoms of Low Motivation

– Labour turnover	– Grievances
– Absenteeism	– Disputes
– Lateness	– Insubordination
– Poor quality	– Low output
– Missing deadlines	– Irresponsibility
– Inconsistency	– Unfriendly service
– Breaking the rules	– Lack of teamwork
– Wastage and errors	– Minimal effort
– Complacency	– Unwillingness

applying ointment to the spots when a child has chickenpox – getting rid of the symptoms doesn't mean they don't have the disease, just that it is less obvious and potentially more threatening. If we accept the view that most people are naturally active, the implication is that something happens to individuals and groups in the work situation to make them less than motivated. And when people are less than content with what they are doing (and according to research at Warwick University some 36 per cent of workers are less than happy with their jobs[1]) they have three possible options. While the obvious choice is to leave and find a more rewarding job elsewhere many people do not feel they have that option because of family commitments or lack of qualifications. Instead they either choose to retire on the job (put in the minimum effort) or redirect their energies into disruption as poor team players or difficult people. Rather than looking for effective ways to control the symptoms it is usually more productive to examine the causes of de-motivation and to identify ways of getting your staff to take more ownership for managing real challenges in their jobs.

PRACTICAL THEORIES OF MOTIVATION

Understanding the true nature of what motivates some people and de-motivates others in similar situations is complex. While there are well-publicised initiatives of companies creating more attractive work environments with enhanced physical conditions and flexible work arrangements, some of the current theories of motivation are a better guide to understanding individual motivation and what to do about de-motivated staff. Four of the more practical theories include Needs Theory, Job Enrichment, Rewards Theory and Climate Theory.

Needs Theory

One of the most popular theories of motivation is Maslow's hierarchy, a general theory which suggests that a great deal of what we do in life is motivated by the desire to satisfy our needs.[2] The contention is that people have needs which in turn create drives to satisfy them through actions taken in their work and personal lives, such as studying for a qualification, seeking promotion, having children, travelling the world or writing a book. Needs theory suggests that if people have little else in their lives the only motivator is the satisfaction of their basic needs such as water, shelter and security. But, as they satisfy those lower order needs, most people move on to higher-level needs, whether for social connection, to be respected by others, to be successful, or to feel that their jobs and their lives have deeper meaning and are worthwhile (see Figure 5.1).

While Maslow's framework indicates an ascending order of needs it further suggests that the only real motivators are the unsatisfied needs – if you already have sufficient food, security or social belonging you are no longer motivated by those needs. Though it may be argued otherwise, most people in jobs today

Figure 5.1: Maslow's Hierarchy of Needs

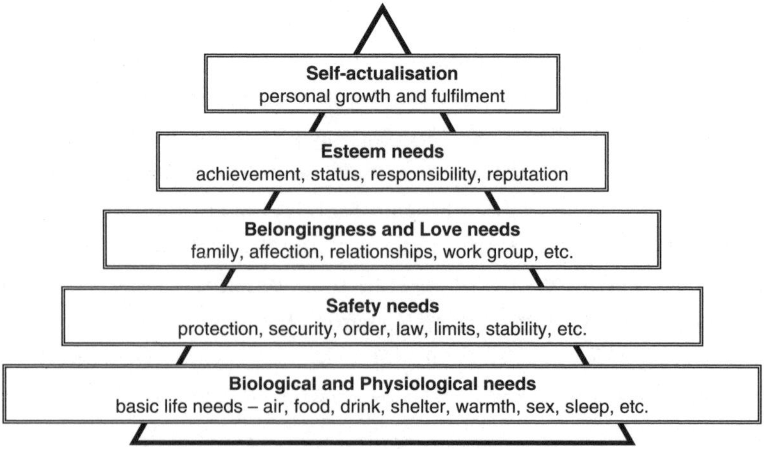

- Self-actualisation: personal growth and fulfilment
- Esteem needs: achievement, status, responsibility, reputation
- Belongingness and Love needs: family, affection, relationships, work group, etc.
- Safety needs: protection, security, order, law, limits, stability, etc.
- Biological and Physiological needs: basic life needs – air, food, drink, shelter, warmth, sex, sleep, etc.

Note: Reproduced with permission from http://www.businessballs.com/maslowhierarchyofneeds5.pdf © Alan Chapman, 2002 have sufficient money to satisfy their basic physical needs and a degree of security through having a pension, savings or saleable skills, and the unsatisfied needs tend to be the higher order needs. But, while most managers are in general agreement with needs theory many still cling to a view that 'increased wages, more security and better working conditions' are what workers want from their jobs even though, according to the theory, for most staff these are already satisfied needs. Several studies show that although managers consistently identify satisfaction of basic needs as the main motivators for staff, when it comes to their own needs they put 'interesting work, a sense of achievement and opportunities for growth and development' top of the list. Even more interesting, is that several studies suggest what workers want from their jobs is almost exactly the same as managers want for themselves.[3]

One rationale for managers continuing to identify their staff with the primary motivators and themselves with the secondary motivators is that the basic needs are more tangible and easier to satisfy. Also they are a common subject of disputes between management and workers and about which unions negotiate (wages, working conditions and security). The most important insight for managers from Malsow's framework is that assuming staff want more of what they already have does not fit well with the theory or the research findings. Some of the conclusions that can be drawn from a practical examination of 'needs theory' are the following:

- While the unsatisfied needs are the main motivators, managers tend to assume their staff want more of what the theory suggests are already satisfied needs.
- Managers rarely ask their staff what they want – instead they operate from a general assumption that staff want more money, better working condition and increased security.
- Different individuals have different needs. While some are motivated by opportunities for training or promotion, others

77

have needs for companionship or a sense of achievement – in order to find out what your staff really want from their jobs you have to consider them as individuals.
- Needs change over time. In early career many young staff are saddled with a large mortgage or want to buy a car and may be energised by the prospect of bonuses and incentives, while in mid-career they may be more interested in promotion or interesting work.
- Managers can influence motivation by identifying the needs of individual staff and helping to satisfy them in the job. In the same way that conflicts in human relationships are often the result of one or both individual's needs not being met, so it is important for managers to discover through discussion or surveys whether de-motivated staff have unrealised or frustrated needs to which they can respond.

Job Enrichment

As a work-related theory Job Enrichment was the outcome of extensive research by Frederick Herzberg and colleagues in which thousands of employees from a variety of organisations were asked to describe an incident or a time in the recent past when they were particularly 'switched on' or 'switched off' by what they were doing. The responses indicated a broad set of categories that included both positive and negative incidents. Further analysis revealed that the things which switched people off (the hygiene factors) were essentially a different set of factors than those that switched them on (the satisfiers): the reason it is sometimes called the two-factor theory[4] (see Figure 5.2).

At a practical level job enrichment suggests that while hygiene factors, such as working conditions or fringe benefits, are important in preventing de-motivation, in the same way that good hygiene can prevent disease, it is the satisfiers that energise people to perform. A second important conclusion is that although the

Figure 5.2: Herzberg Two Factor Theory

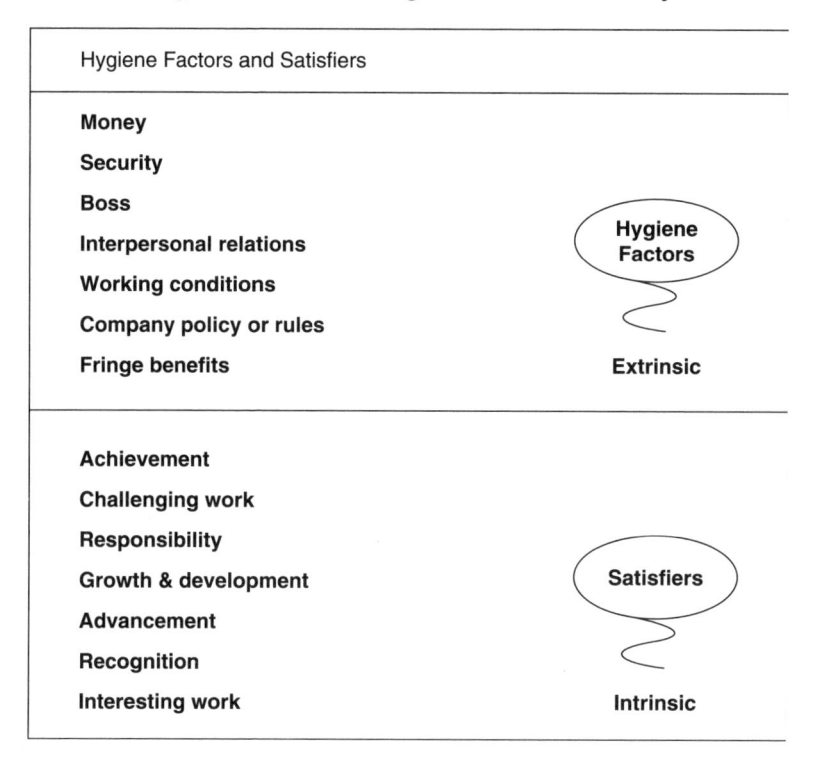

Hygiene Factors and Satisfiers	
Money Security Boss Interpersonal relations Working conditions Company policy or rules Fringe benefits	Hygiene Factors Extrinsic
Achievement **Challenging work** **Responsibility** **Growth & development** **Advancement** **Recognition** **Interesting work**	Satisfiers Intrinsic

hygiene factors tend to be extrinsic (surrounding the job) the true motivators are intrinsic (qualitative characteristics of the work itself). Initial research on job enrichment challenged the assumption that giving people more things to do (job enlargement) was any more motivating than a smaller job, suggesting that the way to energise staff was to vertically load their jobs with satisfiers (job enrichment).

Other researchers, including Scott Myers, elaborated on the work of Herzberg, suggesting that for any job to be 'meaningful' it had to include three elements: Planning, Doing and Control.[5] One example of a meaningful job is the self-employed window cleaner. Not only does he plan his hours, purchase his supplies and canvass territory, but in addition he cleans the windows and at the end of the day can see how much money he has made, knows his costs and has feedback from satisfied customers. As such it is a meaningful job that includes elements of planning, doing and control. However, in the traditional hierarchical organisation the planning and control functions are often taken away from the staff and become the manager's function.

> *Some time ago I worked for a division of a microprocessor company in Silicon Valley where high labour turnover among assembly operators (150 per cent per annum) was effectively killing production. The assembly plant operated a three-shift system and was mainly comprised of female staff. A shortage of skilled labour in the area meant that anyone who was dissatisfied with their job could simply leave and go down the road to one of the many competitors.*
>
> *After some initial data collection and discussion it was clear that one of the main contributors to turnover was the style of the shift supervisors, who tended to be hands-on and controlling, doing everything to remove planning, decision-making and variety away from the operators, but in the process making their jobs less rewarding.*
>
> *It was decided that the way forward was to infuse more planning and control into the assembly jobs. At the front end this was done by establishing clear standards so that each operator knew what was expected of them. Also introduced was individual goal-setting whereby each operator set monthly goals to include both production and personal development. Training sessions were arranged so operators could*

Motivating Staff Beyond Expectations

develop additional skills and opportunities were created for staff to rotate between work stations. At the back end it was agreed that each operator would start to keep their own performance records and that shift performances would in future be made public. In addition the supervisors agreed to carry out a weekly mini-review with each operator and a more formal review of their goals at the end of each month.

While the initiative was greeted enthusiastically by the supervisors and operators alike the implementation process soon began to grind to a halt as the supervisors reluctantly paid lip service to the new approach. Following a management review, it was clear there could be no real benefit for the operators until the supervisor's role became more managerial and they had learned to let go of the hands-on styles with which they were comfortable. Following several initiatives, which included redefining the role of the supervisors, training them in critical interpersonal skills such as how to carry out a job review and termination interview, and encouraging them to set their own goals around improving staff as well as meeting production targets, the benefits began to emerge. Six months later labour turnover was down to a not insignificant but manageable 50 per cent.

As a practical theory job enrichment suggests that some of the critical issues in improving staff motivation include:

- Recognise it is the intrinsic satisfiers that motivate people. While not dismissing the importance of getting the hygiene factors right, increasing the motivation level of staff means finding ways to enrich rather than enlarge their jobs.

- Managers tend to assume that most of their staff have little interest in taking increased responsibility or will only do so in return for money. Rather than involving staff in the process of enriching their jobs Herzberg counselled managers just to start doing it and see the results for themselves.
- Improving motivation means finding simple ways to make jobs more meaningful by vertically loading them with elements of planning and control, including staff having more face-to-face contacts with customers, doing their own troubleshooting, setting goals for self-improvement, reviewing their own performance and keeping their own records

Rewards Theory

Not only are reward and recognition generally recognised as the most powerful short-term motivators, they are also considerably within the gift of the manager. Contrary to a view that it is the organisation which rewards staff, it is clear that most people want recognition from their immediate supervisor, as you know if you have ever worked for a good boss. But, although most managers acknowledge the importance of recognition and are easily convinced that it works well with children and spouses they are generally more comfortable blaming lack of motivation on their inability to provide tangible rewards or improve working conditions. While there is no doubt that money may act as an incentive for people to join an organisation or to stay in the job, studies from both the US and UK show that it takes a substantial rise in pay (over 10 per cent) to produce more effort from an individual and that the motivational effect of a bonus is about six weeks.

> *Money is important to some! After attending a job enrichment seminar a supervisor decided that the suggested techniques could help combat his company's productivity problem. He invited an employee*

> *into his office and told him he would now be allowed to plan, carry out and control his own job. In this way the wanted satisfactions would be introduced into the man's job.*
>
> *The worker asked if he would get more money. The supervisor replied, 'No, money isn't a motivator and you will not be more satisfied if I give you more pay'.*
>
> *Once again the employee asked, 'Well, if I do what you want will I get more pay?' The supervisor answered, 'No, you need to understand motivation theory. Take this book and read it. Tomorrow we'll get together and I'll explain once again what really motivates you.'*
>
> *As the man was leaving he turned back and asked, 'Well, if I read the book will I get more money?'* – Feinberg, *Reader's Digest*.

The role of money as a motivator is confusing in the sense that for some people it may be an incentive or a form of recognition, particularly if the reward relates directly to meeting a specific target or project deadline. For others money may be more about recognising their status or preserving a differential (equity) with other groups. In essence, while it does play a part in motivation the effects of monetary reward are unpredictable, and in some cases can be divisive, as in situations where those who meet their targets or deadlines receive a bonus while those who work equally hard but fail to achieve the results are punished by being denied a reward.

> *I can live for two months on a good compliment*
> – Mark Twain

Rewards theory, or operant conditioning, was initially developed through laboratory experiments with pigeons and rats, where in training animals to complete a task such as jumping through a hoop or ringing a bell the association of a reward with a specific action encouraged them to repeat the behaviour. The principle of reinforcement, popularised in the phrase 'catch people doing things approximately right', suggests that encouraging the efforts of your staff, even if they are not doing things perfectly, is important in developing their confidence and shaping behaviour.

Some practical issues for managers in providing reward and recognition include:

- Identify specific behaviours and attitudes you want to encourage in your staff and find ways to reward them.
- Catch people doing things 'approximately right' rather than exactly right and reward them as an encouragement to stretch themselves.
- Find ways to expand your repertoire of rewards, from thank you notes to public recognition at meetings, celebration of milestones on projects and vouchers or bonuses.
- Understand that most people want recognition from their boss rather than the organisation.
- Personalise rewards by thanking staff in writing with a copy to your boss, recommending staff to others, sending personalised thank you notes and celebrating individual or group successes.

Climate Theory

Most people recognise that the overall atmosphere in which they work has some bearing on their own motivation and the morale of the work group. We have all experienced hotels and shops where the friendliness, energy and efficiency of the staff was clear to all, and visited other establishments where we found the opposite. Much of the positive atmosphere we experience in departments or teams is created by the manager and can have a significant effect on the motivation and morale of their staff.

Although climate is something we sense in a general way, as customers in our positive feelings about a particular restaurant or shop, and as workers in job satisfaction, in reality it is made up of discrete dimensions such as team spirit, commitment, rewards, organisational clarity and friendliness. Each of these dimensions can be measured by asking staff how they feel about those things or carrying out a survey. And more important than using a survey or asking your staff how they experience the climate is that they are involved in analysing the data and agreeing ways to improve the atmosphere.

Some key issues in managing climate:

- It is tempting to assume that others experience the same climate as yourself. Where there are issues relating to de-motivation or lack of commitment the process of involving staff in identifying the causes can be a major step in improving motivation and team morale.
- Get feedback on the current climate, either by asking your staff how they feel (positives and negatives), and how they think the atmosphere could be improved, or by using a standard or tailor-made survey.
- Identify areas for improvement, brainstorm possible actions and invite the staff to share ownership for implementation by assigning individual responsibilities or setting up a task group to take responsibility for improving aspects of the climate.

While the four theories outlined above suggest practical ways for managers to improve motivation they also help explain how staff can become complacent, low in energy and institutionalised. Although most people want meaning, variety and fun in what they do, unless they are working in conditions that sustain their energy they will tend to settle for the comfortable niche of doing the same as yesterday. And while people cannot be motivated against their will, an important part of any manager's function is to create the conditions in which their staff want to perform at their best, or at least not settle for the minimum.

THE POWER OF EXPECTATION

While the main aim of motivation is helping staff to get the best out of themselves, as organisations and managers experience low cost competition and more exacting customer demands, there is increasing pressure to achieve even better results with the same or even less staff. It means not just encouraging staff to give of their best but challenging them to deliver beyond their own expectations of themselves.

Many people, whether at work or in their personal lives, tend to have low or moderate expectations of themselves almost for fear that having challenging ambitions or goals will invite failure. In a fascinating piece of research carried out some years ago, Robert Rosenthal and colleagues conducted a series of experiments on the power of 'expectation'.[6] The initial study with a group of volunteer college students and a number of domestic rats involved half the students being told that they were being given 'maze bright' rats, a more intelligent strain of the rodent that had been developed through a complex programme of scientific inbreeding. In fact the rats were no different than those assigned to the other half of the group who were told that they had been given stupid rats. In a series of experiments the 'maze bright' rats performed significantly better than the other rats.

Reasoning that if the rats were smarter because the students treated them as such, the researchers began to wonder if the same phenomenon might apply in the classroom. They designed a study in which elementary students in a lower-class neighbourhood were given a test that falsely claimed to identify 'intellectual bloomers' in the group. The researchers then randomly selected 20 per cent of the students as 'spurters' who they claimed, on the basis of the test results, had great potential for the future. In fact there was no correlation between their ability and the label. As predicted, eight months later the researchers found the 'spurters' had made marked gains in their reading abilities and achieved significantly higher IQ gains than their peers.

The rationale for the improved performance, according to Rosenthal, was that the teachers unwittingly encouraged greater responsiveness from the students where they expected more. Typically, they suggested, teachers who have high expectations of their pupils raise the bar by giving them more challenging assignments, involving them in projects, asking them more difficult questions and guiding them towards the correct answers.

> *Teachers and leaders share a state secret – that when they expect high performance of their charges they increase the likelihood of high performance* – John Gardner, *On Leadership.*

Since those early experiments, several hundred studies have been carried out in a variety of situations, ranging from increasing the productivity of under-motivated sailors, teaching children to swim and achieving significant improvements in the results of sales people. Collectively they show that a strong belief by managers in the competence of their charges can have a profound effect on motivation because the person's image of themselves affects their performance and further contributes to their own self-concept. According to Livingston[7] the implications of those findings for the average manager can be summed up as follows:

- What managers expect and how they treat their staff can profoundly affect their performance and career progress.
- Good managers create high expectations of their staff that are realistic and achievable.

- Less effective managers have lower expectations of staff and their lack of confidence has an effect on performance.
- Staff tend to do and achieve what they believe is expected of them.

While 'empowerment' has been viewed with some scepticism by commentators as simply a re-labelling exercise, the term does help to focus managers on their ability to raise the expectations of their staff. Current thinking on performance management in relation to stretch goals suggests that encouraging staff to take increased responsibility and share in their manager's concern for broader issues such as quality and service encourages them to live up to the best they can expect of themselves.

> *As conductor of the Boston Philharmonic and corporate consultant, Ben Zander is one who believes that humankind is bedevilled with the constant question, 'am I better or worse than the others?' Those comparisons, he believes, block people from achieving their full potential by making them so anxious about performing well that they are reluctant to take risks in case they fail. As a way of reversing this self-fulfilling prophesy, in his work as a teacher, Zander tells his students on the first day that he has already awarded them an 'A grade' that year and is willing to guarantee them a breakthrough as musicians. The only condition he puts on awarding them the grade is that each student has to submit a letter in the following two weeks written as if it was the end of the year describing how they got the A and where they expect to be at that stage. 'When you give everyone an A', says Zander, 'it changes the nature of the relationship, and I can then teach them to become the person they want to become.'*[8]

Motivating Staff Beyond Expectations

Research carried out with middle managers who were identified as major contributors to innovation and change in their organisation also identifies a supportive boss who provided career challenges and destabilising events as having a significant influence on a person's confidence to take on new and more demanding assignments. Some of the most developmental experiences reported by middle managers include:

- Being encouraged to take on challenging assignments
- Being given early responsibility for tasks beyond their experience
- Being dumped in at the deep end on projects
- Being part of a project team that had to meet a tight deadline
- Tasks that brought them into close contact with senior managers
- Being exposed to a variety of experiences – shifted around
- Being encouraged by their boss to implement their own ideas

However, while some managers intuitively or deliberately communicate high expectations of their staff many others unwittingly communicate low expectations. Whether through being cold and aloof, or focusing on the negatives rather than the positives, they project a lack of expectation that often becomes a self-fulfilling prophecy. And according to Levinson[9] not only do many managers communicate low expectations of their staff but they often believe they are doing otherwise. Argyris agrees with this view, suggesting that while managers are in love with the concept of empowerment, in practice they are much less inclined to let go and encourage their staff because 'the command and control' model is what they are familiar with and continue to trust.[10]

Recently I received an e-mail from the training manager of an organisation where a group of colleagues had completed a series of in-house training programmes.

> *From the written evaluations at the end of each course they identified one participant who felt he had learned nothing from the programme. They forwarded the evaluation form, which interested us all the more when we read it and discovered the response to the question 'Did your boss brief you before you attended?' was an emphatic and capitalised 'NO!!' In a follow-up interview between the training manager and the participant it transpired that he had not been involved in the boss's assessment of his needs and there had been no discussion before he attended the course. Because he came to the programme with the expectation of learning nothing that is exactly what he got – nothing.*

Reversing the 'negative Pygmalion' effect – in which low expectations from their managers can lead to an unwillingness by staff to take on increased responsibility – requires positive steps to include staff in the process of defining objectives for the area, specifying how they might be achieved, agreeing stretch targets and helping them take ownership for their part in making them happen. In that way managers nurture an internal commitment to succeed rather than relying on external incentives to achieve results.

ENRICH ROUTINE AND REPETITIVE WORK

While some managers rationalise the inability to motivate their staff because they can't pay them more money, another common excuse is that the work is itself intrinsically un-motivating. And although some jobs are by their nature routine and repetitive others, over time, can become less challenging as the person masters the job and complacency and disinterest set in. In the same way that managers may need to find ways of preventing their staff from settling into a comfortable routine, they may also need to identify methods for making some of the less intrinsically motivating work more satisfying and energising. A few techniques for re-introducing elements of motivation into more repetitive jobs include:

- Enlarge some jobs by adding variety or increasing the range of skills, such as encouraging staff to become their own problem-solvers, do their own inspections, interface with customers or suppliers, and keep their own records.
- Rotate boring or routine tasks. Many people are willing to do repetitive work as long as it doesn't become their job. Give your staff more discretion by allowing them to self-select for a portion of routine work such as answering the telephones for an hour a day or doing filing for two hours a week. Alternatively, agree that certain jobs can be done at times of the day or week of their choosing.
- Make the routine work more socially attractive. Several early experiments on work design indicate that some people are willing to do repetitive work if it includes elements of social contact or interaction with co-workers or customers, such as telephone interviewing, team packing or group quality inspections.
- Introduce more competition. Appeal to the individual's need for challenge by establishing clear standards on repetitive jobs, setting goals for improvement, publicly tracking output, and rewarding individual and group performance.
- Increase management–staff contacts. Often those who are employed on routine or low-level tasks are left alone unless things go wrong and, as such, are denied the recognition they need from their boss. Support may include scheduling regular work reviews, praising staff for good work, involving them in job- or group-related decisions, personalising awards, managing by wandering around and being available to listen.

Encouraging your staff to take more responsibility for what they are doing means finding ways to get them to perform at or above the current demands of the job. If managers accept that most people are naturally active and want to give their best, then they are responsible for creating the conditions in which their staff can find the energy to perform at that level. At the very least managers need to recognise they may be using styles of managing that are blocking their staff from reaching their full potential and that some of their behaviours may be exacerbating issues of low morale or poor performance. Good parents, teachers, coaches and bosses all show an ability to get the best out of people by encouraging them to perform above their expectations of themselves and that in turn helps to deepen the relationship. Managers acquire staff but they earn enthusiastic and switched-on followers.

CHAPTER 6

Building a Winning Team

Whether comparing restaurants, soccer clubs, hotels or business divisions what we often recognise as key to their effectiveness is teamwork. One of the most memorable hotels I ever stayed in was a Marriott in the Middle East where the skills and interest of the staff clearly suggested a high level of motivation and morale. Several times a day in the elevator or corridor I was asked how I was enjoying my stay and if there was anything they could do to make it more comfortable. My attention was also drawn to the uniform badges worn by each member of staff indicating they were organised into service teams, each dedicated in their own way to making my stay as pleasant as possible. And, following a late breakfast on several mornings I was fascinated to overhear the restaurant manager, in a huddle with his staff, discussing what had gone well and what needed improving at the next sitting. It was teamwork in action and the results were palpable.

LESS PEOPLE – MORE IN TEAMS

In many organisations today there is a very clear need for teamwork. Research indicates that groups which function well as teams are more productive than individuals, while classroom exercises like Lost on the Moon and Desert Survival show that groups make better quality decisions and are more creative than individuals. The benefits of teamwork for some organisations are in increased output or reduced costs, while for others the real payoff is in the softer areas of customer service and team spirit. In addition, many organisations operating in tight labour markets, where it is critical to hang onto experienced staff, realise the benefits of teamwork in improved morale and better staff retention.

> *Teamwork has consistently resulted in greater achievement, productivity, innovation, quality and work satisfaction than 'competitively' driven management environments. This has been demonstrated in studies ranging over scientists, airline reservation agents, business people, students and car assembly workers* – Kharbana and Stalworthy, *Project Teams: The Human Factor.*

Since early initiatives with autonomous work groups in the British coal industry, in companies such as Volvo, and a decade of flirtation with Japanese management, there has been a steady move towards participative styles that emphasise the benefits of people working together in teams. While some groups operate in permanent teams, as in call centres, others work in part-time teams, as with management groups who may need to pull together at key moments to develop strategy and integrate plans. And, in addition to permanent and semi-permanent teams, many staff are members of temporary teams including implementation teams, project teams or quality circles. Teamwork exists in many guises and has become a more regular feature as organisations adopt flatter structures and strive to achieve better results with less people, where the synergies of teamwork and integration are critical.

Building a Winning Team

QUALITIES OF A WINNING TEAM

While developing teamwork can be an important part of the process for letting go to staff the benefits are not so easy to achieve. Calling a group of individuals a team is no guarantee they will work together and poor teamwork may stifle innovation and decision-making. In addition, productivity can also suffer if one or two individuals in the group decide to sit back and let the others do the work.

> *If you have eleven workmen you will never win. If you have eleven artists you will never win. The team has to complement each other. We had that – we had the same vision of football and victory* – Eric Cantona on Manchester United.

So what makes for teamwork and high performing teams? Although it is relatively easy to list the qualities of a good team, as with leadership it is often easier to recognise teamwork when it is absent than when it is present. Think for a moment. When was the last time you were in a group that was not working as a team, whether a project group, a meeting or a work group? What was preventing it from performing well and what needed to happen for it to become a team?

One simple framework that helps to identify the characteristics of effective teams suggests eight places to look for trouble in groups, on the basis that people will naturally work together unless something is blocking them. As the model in Figure 6.1 suggests, all teams, whether temporary or permanent, are simply a group of people who come together to carry out a common task. And groups fall short of becoming teams either because they lack a shared commitment to the task or they fail to realise the synergies of working together. As such, work groups can become

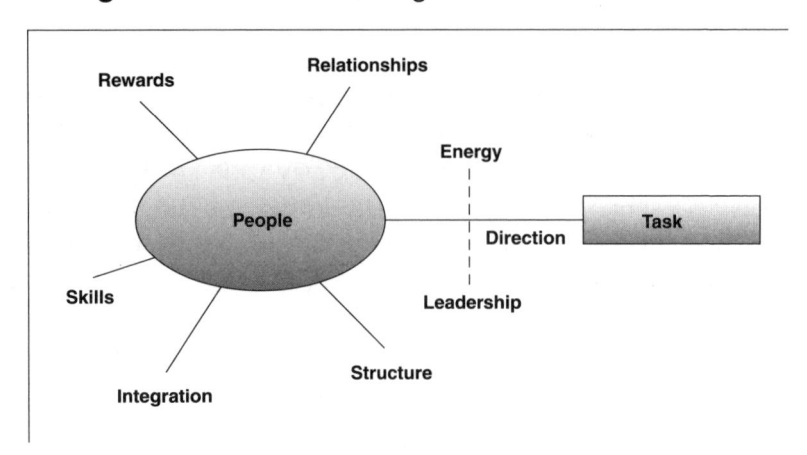

Figure 6.1: Blocks to Organisational Effectiveness

[Diagram: An oval labeled "People" with lines radiating to: Rewards, Relationships, Skills, Integration, Structure, Leadership. A dotted line labeled "Energy / Direction" connects "People" to a box labeled "Task".]

blocked from realising their potential for any combination of the following reasons:[1]

1. *Lack of Direction* – for any group to become an effective team requires a shared sense of commitment to what they want to achieve, variously defined as a purpose, vision, mission or strategic objectives. A group of individuals with widely differing views on what they are trying to build will inevitably create division. Even regular meetings can lose sight of what they were set up to deliver or the purpose they continue to serve.
2. *Low Energy* – although members of a group may have a great deal of commitment to what they are doing as individuals the energy of the group can sometimes be dissipated through distraction, shifting priorities and administrative bureaucracy. And groups often fail to realise the benefits of teamwork because some individuals are so preoccupied with their own jobs they lose sight of the purpose, priorities or goals of the team. In addition, groups also lose energy over time if they

are not continually renewing their focus through finding new challenges to fuel their commitment to each other and the future.
3. *Inappropriate Structures* – while the operating structures within any team should act as a support to getting the work done and help to keep the group together, sometimes vague and ambiguous job roles, unclear reporting relationships or too many reporting levels can inhibit teamwork. Do individuals in the team know what is expected of them? Do they understand their function within the group? Do their workloads, targets or reporting relationships discourage cooperation and synergy?
4. *Poor Relationships* – working well as a team requires a significant level of trust between members of the group. Mistrust can result in individuals guarding information, the development of self-serving cliques and a reluctance to value the contribution of others. Building a level of trust that supports teamwork is conditional on people feeling free to be open and honest with each other and sharing feedback in constructive ways. It may also mean developing processes that allow issues from the past to get surfaced and dealt with, such as interpersonal conflicts, unbalanced workloads or dysfunctional role boundaries. Is there sufficient trust in the group, and a willingness to share information and to be open and honest with each other?
5. *Inadequate Rewards* – do members of the team feel they are sufficiently recognised for their contribution to the team, not so much in financial terms but in involvement and consultation? Is the package of rewards available to team members sufficiently varied and fairly administered? Effective teamwork requires that individuals are rewarded for their contribution to group performance rather than simply for individual results which may encourage unhealthy competition and divisiveness.
6. *Skill Gaps* – no matter how good the team effort, if there is a deficit in individual or group competencies it may be difficult to realise the synergies of teamwork. Models of team development

such as Belbin's Team Roles suggest that while groups may aspire to work as a team they often lack the right mix of technical or social skills needed to function well together.[2] And apart from individual skills, group competencies often define a team's overall effectiveness, such as their ability to manage consensus, create flexible work arrangements, provide a consistent service or develop team spirit.

7. *Insufficient Integration* – while they may understand their individual roles and functions, one potential block to teamwork is poor integration. Sometimes the fault lies in a lack of appreciation of each other's work and contribution, or to interdisciplinary conflicts from the past. In other situations the absence of mechanisms to coordinate the effort may be an essential block,

Table 6.1: Rate Your Work Group as a Team

1. Direction – is there a clear and shared commitment to the team and what is it there to achieve?
2. Energy – is the energy of the team high and focused on what you are trying to achieve?
3. Structure – are roles and reporting relationships clear and are they supporting or blocking the team?
4. Relationships – are members of the team open and honest with each other? What level of trust is there in the group? Are there unresolved issues?
5. Rewards – are individuals adequately recognised for their contribution to the team? Are the rewards fair and effective?
6. Skills – are the right people in the right places? Does the team have the right competencies to operate as an effective team?
7. Integration – are mechanisms in place to encourage communication and cooperation between members of the group?
8. Leadership – is there a shared sense of leadership in the team. Is it focused and proactive?

such as the lack of team meetings or meetings that fail to address the real issues, an absence of policies or integrating roles, while poor communications and conflict management skills can also be critical barriers to team effectiveness.
8. *Lack of Leadership* – while research has established that well-functioning and committed teams generally achieve better results than individuals, and that most people do want to work as part of a team, it takes good leadership to manage the potential blocks. And the need for effective leadership is not confined to the manager or project leader but must be shared by all members taking responsibility in pushing for team improvement and keeping the group focused on the task.

USE THE TEAM TO IMPROVE TEAMWORK

No matter how well people are working as a team there is always room for improvement and a need for constant maintenance. In most work groups it is probably safe to assume:

- There are hidden agendas
- There is under-communication
- There are dysfunctional norms
- There is insufficient trust
- There is less synergy than possible
- There are unresolved conflicts

While an obvious step to better teamwork is agreeing an action plan for improvement, it is often best to start by examining the present level of functioning in the group. And while it may be tempting to use questionnaires or gather information there may be some benefit in involving the whole group in the process.

One simple exercise that provides a good introduction to teambuilding is 'Prouds and Sorrys'. If your team is larger than eight people consider dividing them into two groups and allow twenty minutes for the groups to draw up a list of the things they are Proud of in relation to the team and a similar list of things about which they are Sorry. Now, ask them to identify two things from each side they would have some energy to work on over the next three months and allow them fifteen minutes to draw up a short-term action plan. Another approach, aimed at improving interpersonal relationships in a team, is the 'Johari window', so called because it is a four-box model developed by Joe Luft and Harry Ingham[3] (see Figure 6.2). The model suggests that while part of each person is on Public display to the group other aspects of their behaviour are either Blind to them, Hidden from the other team members or in their unconscious, Unknown to them and only accessible through counselling or therapy.

The Johari window suggests that relationships within a team can be improved by reducing either the Hidden side through encouraging individuals to be more open with their colleagues or the Blind side by giving feedback to each other. In teambuilding not only does the Johari model present a simple and credible framework for understanding relationships, it also suggests the benefits of encouraging more openness in the team, of individuals exploring their contribution to the group and the value of honest feedback.

As a practical option for sharing feedback and promoting openness consider introducing a routine where members of the

Figure 6.2: Johari Window

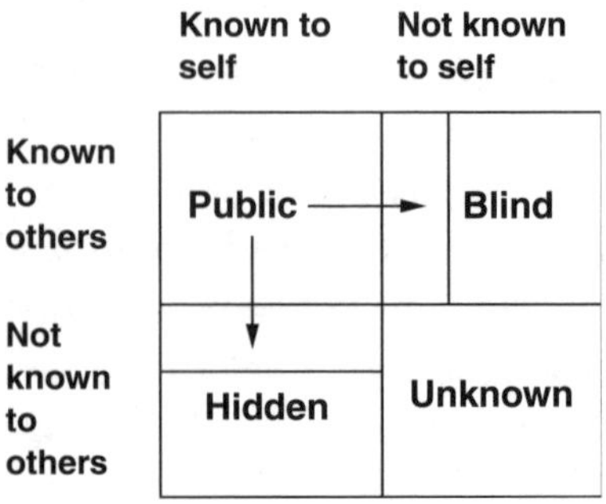

	Known to self	Not known to self
Known to others	Public	Blind
Not known to others	Hidden	Unknown

group are invited to give each other feedback in open session. Occasionally, at the end of a team meeting or off site session, take some time to put each individual in focus for three or four minutes and invite the others, in turn, to give them feedback. Ensure that at least one piece of feedback is positive, such as 'what you contribute most to the team', and one corrective piece, such as 'what I would like to see you do more or less of in the team'. Establish a ground rule that when each person is in focus they simply thank the other for the feedback rather than feeling a need to respond or explain, and at the end invite each person to summarise what they think they heard and intend to do differently for the future.

Also useful in examining the current level of team functioning is to revisit the shared vision as a way of re-energising staff beyond their individual jobs. One design involves each member of the group drawing a picture, diagram or flow chart of how they see the department currently and how they would like to see it in three years time. Provide pens and half a sheet of flip chart paper for each person and encourage them to be creative. When they have finished, display the drawings on the wall and give each person a few minutes to describe their picture to the others. Discuss possible linkages between the drawings and brainstorm what needs to be done to move towards a shared vision for the future. As a first step in the process, ask a couple of staff to write a one-page report on what came out of the exercise and circulate it for future discussion.

ENCOURAGE TEAM TALK

In the same way that families often co-exist at a superficial level, so work groups are frequently reluctant or unable to raise and deal with the real issues that are blocking them from working effectively as a team. Especially where the group has been together for a while any teambuilding process should include opportunities to raise and deal with the less comfortable issues that may be blocking

Figure 6.3:   Overt/Covert Triangle

Overt — Discussable

- Strategy
- Systems
- Technology
- Structure

- Work practices
- Climate
- Norms
- Trust
- Interpersonal conflicts

Covert — Undiscussable

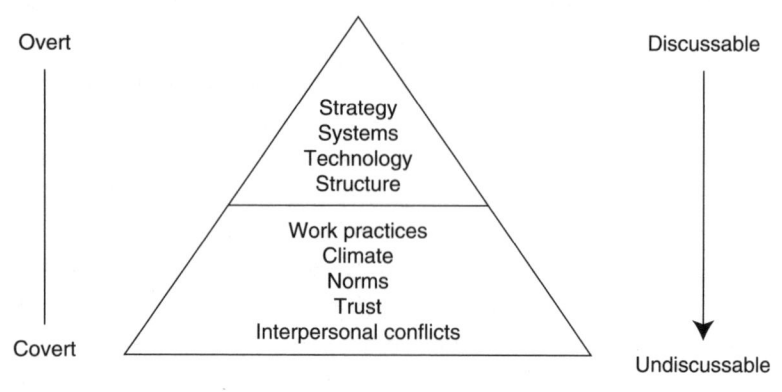

them. Though groups are generally willing to talk about tangible blocks to teamwork such as administrative procedures or the team structure, they are often less forthcoming when it comes to confronting issues like dysfunctional work norms, unequal workloads, lack of participation, mistrust, the manager's style or legacies from the past that have become undiscussable (see Figure 6.3). One way of raising their consciousness about the less discussable issues in the group is to open them up at one-on-one reviews or informal chats, particularly if you sense they are inhibiting team performance.

MEETINGS AS MICROCOSMS

One place that individuals frequently come together in teams is at meetings. Whether temporary meetings, as with project teams, or regular team meetings they often reveal, in microcosm, the life of a group and how well people are working outside the meeting. As with work teams, dysfunctional norms and unresolved conflicts are rarely raised and dealt with, no matter how ineffective the meeting is at achieving its objectives or satisfying the needs of the group.

While some meetings are essentially about sharing information and others for making decisions the objective of most meetings is to reach consensus, on the basis that two heads are better than one and a meeting of minds is often more important than getting the best result. Yet at meetings people often launch into the agenda without clarifying the purpose of the meeting or the expected outputs. And meetings sometimes fail to deliver what they promise because the procedures for managing them have not been agreed, such as how the agenda will be compiled and managed, who will take the minutes, the length of the meeting, or when and by whom action items will be progressed.

However, meetings also get into trouble for less overt reasons, either through developing dysfunctional norms such as allowing certain individuals to dominate the discussion, those with the best information not being heard, or some people staying quiet because they fear being misunderstood. In a seminal article based on the Bay of Pigs incident where a US cabinet, headed by President John F. Kennedy, supported Cuban refugees in their abortive invasion of Cuba, the author questions how they could have made a decision that in Kennedy's words was 'so stupid'. Having studied many similar decisions author Irving Janis concludes that groups have a tendency to become victims to what he terms 'groupthink'.[4]

As with permanent teams it is common for meetings to develop norms or habits that are aimed at maintaining cohesiveness in the group rather than contributing to its effectiveness. Janis discovered that groups often make quick decisions because they fear their indecisiveness and, once made, defend the fragile consensus against anyone who disagrees. The movie *Twelve Angry Men*, a courtroom drama in which Henry Fonda managed to sway eleven jurors from their guilty verdict in a murder case, showed that although his doggedness helped to reverse the decision he made few friends in the process. In reality, not only do those who disagree with the majority view at meetings often fail to speak up for fear of breaking the apparent consensus, but complacency and group pressure also come into play. Concluding that the benefits of working in groups are often lost because powerful psychological pressures intervene, particularly when members share the same values and experiences, the author suggests that groups may need to encourage rather than suppress their disagreements and doubts.

> *The Abilene Paradox, a classic management parable, illustrates how groups can sometimes make misguided decisions because no one is willing to raise objections against what they see as the majority view. It concerns a couple and their in-laws who on one hot and clammy afternoon in Coleman, Texas are comfortably playing dominoes on the porch when the father-in-law suggests they drive to Abilene for dinner. His wife says it is a great idea and the others, one by one, go along with the decision. The long drive is both dusty and hot, the food in the cafeteria is inedible and they arrive back some four hours later, exhausted.*
>
> *Having recovered from their ordeal they begin to question the decision, the mother-in-law admitting that she would rather have stayed at home but felt pressured to go along with the rest. The others also began to admit that they went along to be sociable and because they thought everyone else was in agreement and they didn't want to alienate themselves. 'Here we were four reasonable people who, of our own volition, had just taken a 106-mile trip across a godforsaken desert in furnace-like heat and a dust storm to eat unpalatable food at a hole-in-the-wall diner in Abilene, when none of us wanted to go. To be concise we'd done just the opposite of what we wanted to do'.*[5]

While meetings often suffer from similar blocks as work groups they also provide opportunities for team development through illustrating that what goes wrong at meetings is often reflected in the work group. Meetings typically get into trouble at four levels:[6]

- Purpose
- People
- Procedures
- Process

Sometimes the Purpose of a meeting may be unclear in terms of the reason it is being held or what it is trying to achieve, while on other occasions those People attending are unclear about their role in terms of what they are expected to contribute – 'am I here to represent my area or express a personal opinion?' and 'do I contribute to agenda items that don't affect me?' Often what frustrates people about meetings is the absence of clear Procedures such as preparatory material, a finishing time, a clear agenda or agreed follow-up. And while they may aspire to consensus, meetings often end up in a compromise of winners and losers because the Process is badly managed. As a consequence some meetings dissolve into interpersonal disagreements or railroading and others are too polite or non-confronting to achieve an open and honest exchange of views.

Managing consensus at meetings requires two important ingredients: firstly, that individuals are encouraged to share their knowledge and listen to each other and, secondly, that people challenge the facts and assumptions frequently made in groups. Although they may lack information, rarely does it prevent people expressing trenchant views as if they were facts. As a result meetings often end up pooling the participants' ignorance rather than sharing their knowledge. Also at meetings people often make wild assumptions that go unchallenged, such as the cost of a proposal, the time it will take to complete a project or how acceptable a decision will be to those affected. In the final analysis, some meetings end up as 'fat and happy', while others are challenging, but those with the best information are listened to the least.

How well meetings function can be explored in a number of ways, one is by taking occasional time-outs to check how the meeting is going. It gives those attending an opportunity to challenge the meeting having drifted from its purpose or agenda, whether some people are dominating the discussion or others are not being heard. Another simple discipline at the end of meetings is to take a few minutes to review the process, getting each person to rate the meeting under a number of headings such as:

Was the meeting... (rate 1–10)

- Focused?
- Productive?
- Enjoyable?
- Open?
- Challenging?
- Inclusive?

When the individual scores have been collated it is usually easy to see where the meeting is being blocked, and this in turn makes it more acceptable for individuals to be specific in their comments. While it may be useful to follow up the exercise with a short brainstorming session on how the meeting could be improved, it is sometimes more productive to assign one person at each meeting to the role of process observer. Apart from contributing to the meeting in the normal way their job is to give feedback at the end of the meeting, to intervene whenever they feel the group has drifted from the topic, and to signal when individuals are staying silent or the meeting is being railroaded by a few individuals. In meetings, as in work groups, the process itself is often the real product in the sense that how well people work together often determines the results they achieve. And working together as a well-integrated and focused team usually gets better results than working as individuals.

CREATIVE WAYS TO IMPROVE TEAMWORK

One of the main problems with teams is that as they mature they can become complacent and set in their ways. Sometimes low energy stems from getting into a routine, at other times because people contrive to support or at least not to hurt each other, and as a result there is insufficient challenge. One way of preventing complacency is to take time out to review the working of the group, whether through surveys or occasional team-building sessions. But, on the assumption that all teams eventually reach a stage of maturity it can be useful, now and again, to identify ways of preventing low energy and group burnout. Some creative ideas for keeping a work group fresh in ideas and renewing their challenge as a team include:

1. Vary the location of meetings. Have you noticed that when people get together at routine meetings they often sit in the same places and a similar dynamic repeats itself? Try changing the dress code for some meetings, or meet in a different venue or at a different time. Get people to change places occasionally or have breakaways into smaller groups before opening up a topic for more general discussion. Have occasional meetings where there is no agenda and the purpose is to review how well the group is working. And, apart from energising your regular meetings, plan to take time-outs for more studied sessions to examine major blocks to teamwork and ways of improving group functioning.
2. Have good news meetings. One of the unintended consequences of team meetings is the tendency to focus on what is going wrong rather than on the positives. It can have a negative effect on team morale and lead to norms of criticism and cynicism

rather than respect and celebration. If there is a tendency for the agenda of your meetings to reflect a mainly negative view consider introducing a norm that at least 50 per cent must be about what is going right. Also, give team members an occasional opportunity to brag about their individual achievements by asking them to do mini-presentations on projects, report on the work of their task group or plan to circulate good news to other teams.

3. Work on shared challenges. It is sometimes interesting to observe how people rally round when there is a family crisis. Not only do they immediately identify with a shared need but they also want to do their bit to help. One way of re-energising a team is finding a new challenge, whether to achieve a safety or hygiene award, meet a tight budget or beat the competition. Similar challenges can also energise a team around softer values such as customer service or quality. Consider setting up a task group to clarify the team's values on quality, care or service, and assign members to the team who may not have previously taken that level of responsibility. It is fascinating to observe the way that some individuals, cast as average team players, respond when they are given a new level of responsibility and a clear challenge to deliver.

4. Use Brainstorming. As a way of breaking the routine of meetings have an occasional freewheeling or brainstorming sessions to liven things up. One variation is known as Open Systems Technology (OST). Start by asking each member of the group to write down an issue or concern they would like to debate at the team meeting and make them public, on post-it notes or a whiteboard. Collate the issues and get the group to select the two or three they would most like to include on the agenda for the meeting. An alternative to OST is Brainstorming, which takes a specific issue or problem, such as how to streamline the administration system, how to reduce customer complaints, rework or production bottlenecks. At the start of

the session remind participants of the three key rules in brainstorming: firstly, the more ideas the better; secondly, the person with the pen does not edit the ideas; and thirdly, the more creative the ideas the better.

A short period of time is then given for each group to generate as many ideas as possible for resolving the issue. Each group is then asked to identify the most practical suggestions on the list and the maddest or most creative. Sometimes it is the most bizarre or apparently impractical idea that contains the seed of a possible solution.

An energy company in North America was experiencing problems with ice building up on their power lines during the harsh winters that were costing a fortune in repairs and seriously affecting customer service. Representatives from several disciplines and departments met to brainstorm the problem of how to encourage rid of the ice. One linesman who had had encountered bears when repairing the lines suggested they encourage bears to climb the poles and shake off the ice, while another suggested they attach honey pots to the lines to attract the bears. The somewhat bizarre image of a 'bear in the air' suggested the possibility of using the powerful down draft of a helicopter to dislodge the ice. That relatively simple solution eventually saved the company thousands of dollars a year in reduced repairs and unbroken service.

Although brainstorming has been around for some time, and is used extensively in advertising and design, it is also a useful technique for getting groups of staff involved and energised about resolving issues that may be seen as intractable. While it can be used as a stand-alone technique it can also be usefully included as part of a meeting or off site.

Hanging On and Letting Go: The Art of Real Delegation

5. Have brown bag sessions. Within any work group there is usually a great deal of knowledge that for one reason or another is not shared. And it is often lack of information about what each other is doing that leads to mistrust and lack of openness. Having to make a short presentation to colleagues on aspects of your work or a personal project is a potential motivator and mechanism for reward. Brown bag sessions are so called because they are generally at lunchtime, consist of a few short presentations and discussion, accompanied by a sandwich lunch.

6. Team training. Most staff can expect to be schooled in the skills that relate to their own jobs, but are rarely offered training in how to be a good team player. And while periodic job or role reviews can promote better teamwork it also helps if group members have a better understanding of what makes for an effective team. Diagnostic instruments such as 360 degree feedback and role analysis can help individuals recognise their place and contribution to the team while exercises such business simulations, outdoors development, consensual problem-solving or group projects can also assist in identifying the dynamics of effective teamwork.

Not all groups are teams, and teams are sometimes only teams for part of the time. Professional golfers, who mostly play as individuals, when selected for events such as the Ryder Cup become part of a highly motivated team thanks to the leadership of an acknowledged captain and a clear and inspiring challenge. But whether they are in temporary task groups, permanent work teams or regular meetings, achieving the benefits of teamwork is increasingly important for four reasons.

Firstly, thanks to technology replacing many routine and semi-skilled operations more and more groups are made up of knowledge workers. As such their jobs are less specific, more interdependent and their performance is dependent on sharing knowledge with others. Secondly, as organisations are increasingly sensitised by the changing environment to the needs of customers and the competition there are obvious benefits in having a team approach where individuals make consistent responses as needs arise. Thirdly, there is convincing data that well-functioning teams produce better results than individuals, not only in the hard areas of meeting targets and deadlines, but in the softer areas like service, quality, friendliness and integrity. And finally, the use of temporary teams during change programmes, whether as quality circles, implementation groups or customer service teams, illustrates the potential benefits of the teamwork approach.

As leader of a work group it is the responsibility of every manager to get the best out of their people, both as individuals when individual performance is needed and as a team when a team approach is required. While your staff may want to be part of a challenging and successful work group many things conspire to get in the way of them operating as a team. Building a winning team that is focused on its mission and self-managed in many aspects of its functioning is one of the best ways of letting go to others and for ensuring they get more than just a sense of individual achievement in the job.

CHAPTER 7

Dealing with Problem Staff

At some point in every manager's career they are likely to inherit or recruit someone who ends up being difficult to handle. Problem staff are in plentiful supply – it is estimated that one in six employees is seen as difficult by their colleagues or boss and, who knows, at some stage of your career you may have been one of those problem people! Not only can difficult staff take up a great deal of a manager's time, reportedly as much as 50–60 per cent, but they can also have a significant effect on the rest of the staff.

So, where to begin with managing problem staff? Firstly, it helps if you react in ways that are less likely to result in the person becoming even more of a problem. While the natural reaction is to avoid them as a way of minimising your own stress, or in the hope that they will get the message, it rarely works. As with difficult children it often exacerbates the problem, the incidents being less frequent but more dramatic. Secondly, managers can spend a great deal of time analysing why a problem person is acting the way they are and viewing them as being deliberately difficult. While it may be natural to look for possible reasons, as with any analysis of human behaviour you may be right but equally well you could be wrong. Often people themselves don't know why they are difficult and even if your analysis is right what then? Thirdly, the habit of attaching labels to problem staff such as lazy, devious, thoughtless or stupid is equally unhelpful. Not only does it make it hard to see beyond the label, but as author Brendan Kennelly comments, 'labelling people is the way we dehumanise them', suggesting that it is much easier to deal with a label than trying to relate to the person as a person.

In addition, not only are managers inclined to avoid, analyse and label problem staff, but they often overreact in those situations because difficult people have the effect of deskilling them. All the skills and techniques that work so well with other people often fail to have the same effect with difficult staff, and as a result managers are inclined to become defensive and difficult in return. In effect the manager can become a difficult person for their problem staff.

ANOTHER VIEW OF DIFFICULT PEOPLE

While it may be tempting to see some individuals as deliberately difficult, in reality there is no such thing as problem people, only people with problems. Not alone do most staff want to perform well at work and go home at the end of the day feeling good about themselves but it is also hard work being difficult. Most problem staff are less than happy and many are low in self-esteem. You may remember a time in your own life when you felt less than good about yourself, as a confused adolescent with your parents, going through a difficult patch in a relationship or having fractious disputes with your children. In all likelihood you were less than happy, wished those confrontations hadn't taken place, and in moments of quiet reflection blamed yourself for at least being part of the problem.

The most positive read of difficult staff is that they are coping with stress in the only way they know how. When people are under pressure, whether at work or in their personal lives, they typically react in one of two ways, either by running away from the stress or standing and fighting. Popularly known as the flight/fight syndrome, it is a primitive response to stress, its origins in a time when people faced physical dangers from wild animals or a well-armed enemy. In those circumstances they had to make quick decisions, either to remove themselves rapidly or stand and face the threat.

Although we are engineered to respond to occasional periods of heightened stress in our lives and can sometimes find amazing physical and emotional resources when there is a crisis, if that level of stress continues over time it may become a chronic condition in which the individual over-reacts to the slightest challenge and as such becomes hard to live with or difficult to manage.

STRATEGIES WITH PROBLEM STAFF

While there are no instant remedies for managing difficult people there are a number of strategies for challenging them or dealing with the consequences of their behaviour in productive ways. An initial approach is to look for a cause, particularly where the person has a good work record and has only recently become difficult to manage. A second initial strategy is to confront the issue. Here it is important to focus on the problem rather than the person. You are not trying to change the individual's personality, just the way they respond to particular situations or conditions.

A medium-term strategy for dealing with problem staff is to look for better ways to cope with their behaviour or the effect it has on others and in doing so to focus on improving a relationship which may have deteriorated over time. Finally, a longer-term strategy is to look for more solid ways of changing their job or the situation in which you both find yourselves.

The Four C's in dealing with difficult staff include:

1. Counsel them to identify the cause
2. Confront the issue or the problem

3. Cope with the effects on the relationship
4. Change the job or the situation

COUNSEL THE CAUSE

Frequently an individual's unacceptable behaviour or poor performance can be identified with a specific incident in the past or present. If their attitude or behaviour has generally been positive and the deterioration can be traced to a specific incident, such as a negative job review or a personal dispute, rather than avoiding the issue in the hope they will eventually see reason use it as an opportunity to strengthen the relationship. Make time to find out how they see and feel about the issue and give them feedback on how you see the problem. Let them know how their behaviour is affecting you and others, and show a willingness to help in resolving the issue.

One of the keys to effective counselling is keeping ownership of the issue with the individual. Rather than collecting information from the person, which may create an expectation that you are going to resolve things, listen with the intention of getting them to acknowledge and confront their unacceptable behaviour or poor performance. As well as helping them listen to themselves also encourage them to suggest possible solutions or options for resolving the impasse, and rather than pushing for a complete resolution agree a few first steps and a way in which you will jointly monitor progress.

While focusing on the cause of the behaviour is a primary strategy it generally applies only in situations where the problem person has a past history as a good performer and their work or behaviour has deteriorated in recent times. On more deep-seated issues a cause is less likely – even they may not know what is making them act as they are, and analysing 'why' can take up a great deal of time and fail to suggest any remedies.

CONFRONT THEIR BEHAVIOUR

Where a member of staff has been difficult over time, during periods of work pressure or with others, it is important to confront their behaviour. Ignoring the consequences of their actions or trying to smooth things over generally leads to even more extreme reactions. It is usually best to work on the premise that no one is deliberately difficult and most difficult people are responding to stress in the only way they know how. Start by identifying their behaviour as mainly passive or aggressive. Under pressure some people externalise their stress by reacting in aggressive ways towards others, such as irritability, anger, blaming, disruption, negativism or impulsive behaviour (see Table 7.1).

While aggressives tend to externalise their stress, passives do the opposite, turning their stress inwards in moodiness, anxiety or dependency. And sometimes passives literally run away from work pressures through illness, absenteeism or chronic lateness. While some passives exhibit classic traits associated with poor self-esteem, including putting themselves down, being unwilling to accept responsibility or wanting others to make their decisions,

Table 7.1: Types of Difficult Behaviour

Aggressive	Passive
Insubordination	Self-doubt
Blaming	Indecision
Anger, Rage	Depression
Disruptive behaviour	Rigidity
Cynicism	Dependency
Passive aggression	Anxiety
Negativism	Hypochondria
Denial	Moodiness
Paranoia	Lateness/absenteeism

aggressives also react to a poor self-image but in more overt ways such as bullying, disruption and argument.

Example 1:

> Jim inherited a secretary who in normal circumstances was easy to work with. But when there was any degree of pressure (which was in the nature of the business) she became moody, critical to his face and badmouthed him to others, blaming her inability to meet deadlines on poor planning and lack of consideration for her workload. Unfortunately those were also the times he was most under pressure, which added to his stress and the morale of the team. These episodes were frequently followed by a few days of absence and an accompanying doctor's note, which implied that her illness was a result of the pressure she was being placed under at work.

Example 2:

> Anne identifies one of her staff as constantly on the defensive, seeing every action as deliberately aimed against her. A typical incident involved a decision made by management to dispense with daily reports and to track stock as it came into the warehouse. It was agreed that it would be her job to print off the stock sheet, check her own inventory and pass the sheet on. She immediately saw this as in some way diminishing her role and refused. When it was eventually decided to bypass her she immediately produced a doctor's certificate claiming that the noise of the printer, located in her office, was causing severe headaches.

Example 3:

> John has a member of staff who alternates from being supportive to becoming negative and snappy. An extremely territorial person, he is unwilling to share the workload even when he is under pressure, choosing to work long hours rather than give any of his work to colleagues. 'If I mention that I have asked someone to do something that he considers part of his job he says "OK" and walks away, dismissing me as if I had been disloyal. If I try to explain he avoids me for days at a time. It is always me who has to reconnect.'

While it is useful in confronting difficult staff to identify them as passive or aggressive, in reality it is a continuum of behaviours, some individuals reacting in classically aggressive or passive ways while others display passive aggressive behaviour, such as angry responses followed by long periods of silence, and others alternate between both: sometimes overtly difficult and at other times moody and temperamental. However, the main reason for identifying problem staff as mainly one or the other is that the approaches to confronting aggressives are essentially different from working with passives (see Table 7.2).

When confronting aggressives 'push' tactics are required. As with most bullies their preferred or learned way of dealing with

Hanging On and Letting Go: The Art of Real Delegation

Table 7.2: Confronting Tactics

Aggressives – Use Push Tactics	**Passives – Use Pull Tactics**
– Stop them/slow them down – Give them feedback/ facts and feelings – State expectations – let them know what you want and don't want from them – Be firm – don't back down on your position – Keep ownership with them – Set goals for improvement/change – Be clear about what you want – put it in writing – Monitor their behaviour closely	– Show a willingness to listen to their side of things – Use open questions to draw them out – Reflect back what they are saying and the emotions behind it – Help them confront their concerns and emotions – Give them positive feedback – Reinforce the good bits of their performance/ behaviour – Get them to focus on a positive outcome – Have frequent contacts – Agree minimal change

stress is to externalise it onto others with a raised voice, menace or dogmatism. The main tactics include staying adult when they raise their voice, stopping them – 'let me just stop you there' – slowing them down by using frequent summaries, looking for clarification and letting them know what you will and will not accept.

Confronting passives essentially requires 'pull' approaches, which include showing a willingness to listen, encouraging them to talk about their feelings, reflecting back the emotion as well as the content, giving them recognition for what they do well and agreeing first steps rather than overwhelming them with the need for improvement or change.

Dealing with Problem Staff

While it is tempting to ignore or smooth over the effects of problem staff, what often prevents managers from confronting them is a history of failed attempts in the past – and there is nothing like failure to undermine your own self-confidence. Negative experiences with difficult staff usually result from getting into the same scripts or dialogues that end in raised voices, standoffs or further distancing from the other person. And, while it may not be possible to change their reaction to being confronted it is possible to change your approach and in so doing achieve a better response.

> *In a classroom exercise participants are asked to identify someone who for them is a problem person. After sharing their cases the group selects one that sounds particularly interesting. With that person playing themselves and someone from the group playing the difficult person a role-play situation is set up as realistically as possible according to whether a typical incident takes place on the phone, in an office or on the corridor. The two role-players then engage in a four-minute role-play. After the first role-play the group discusses what happened, brainstorms some better options for dealing with the situation and agrees another approach. The same role-player uses the new approach and at the end of the second session the group again reviews the result and agrees an alternative approach. Invariably, after three short role-plays there is a much different and more confident process in play, and a considerably better result.*

A simple adage in communications that 'intention is nothing, results are everything' makes a great deal of sense in dealing with many interpersonal situations. No matter how well you think you performed at a job interview or how effectively you pitched that proposal, if you didn't get the job or win the project it was an unsuccessful piece of communication. It follows that if what you are doing now isn't getting you what you want, one option is to try something else, and in doing so you often achieve a better result. While you may feel you have little control over the behaviour or performance of a member your staff, what you do have some choice about is your approach and how you choose to react to them.

> *Some years ago I ran a series of residential courses for newly appointed Training Officers from local government. It was a four-week-long residential course with a gap of a month in the middle during which participants completed a project. On the first morning of one course, as I asked participants to introduce themselves, I had a frosty reception from a participant who continued in the same vein with audible criticism and an unwillingness to participate in exercises she thought were 'silly'. As a result I avoided her as much as possible and she was not included by the other participants in their social events. Her general negativism reached a point towards the end of the first part of the programme that left me little option but to confront the issue. Taking her to one side I suggested that she consider whether to return for the second half of the course, and while agreeing that she wasn't enjoying the programme her main concern was how her boss and the local authority would react.*
>
> *Part of the programme included my visiting each participant to coach them on their new function and review their projects. On the way to meet her I*

decided to take a different approach. Although I received the anticipated cool reception I focused on the good bits of her project and listened to how she felt about the first part of the programme. It ended up being a positive visit and, to her credit, she had done a useful project.

On her return I was able to highlight her project as a good example and went out of my way to spend more time with her and ensure that she was included in social events. It elicited an entirely different response. From being my main critic she became my chief ally and by the end of the course most of the participants had also warmed to her. The episode is a constant reminder that changing your reaction to difficult people is often enough to change their behaviour.

COPE WITH THE RELATIONSHIP

While confronting problem staff may improve the immediate situation, in the medium-term it may be important to find ways of improving the relationship. Often relationships get into trouble because there is a mismatch between what the other person wants from us and what we expect from them. Finding common ground where you can both get what you want may help move you towards a more productive relationship.

One expectation that sometimes creates a rift between individual staff and their boss is the way they are managed. As the leadership model outlined in Chapter 2 suggests, while managers may have a preferred style of working with staff it may frustrate some from realising their potential or jar with their expectation of how they should be managed. In the same way that parents who closely supervise their children into adolescence sometimes find they end up doing exactly what their parents most fear, so not all staff respond in the same way to a particular style of leadership.

In terms of changing the relationship, rather than spending a great deal of time analysing your style, start by identifying a few simple things you could do differently. Try being a bit less hands-on with that person, which is what we are inclined to do with poor performers. Adopt a more coaching style, encouraging them to find their own solutions to work issues or at least keeping ownership with them. Also, on the basis that we are inclined to put distance between ourselves and difficult people start to schedule more frequent contacts. Make a point of touching base more frequently or schedule regular one-on-one work reviews as part of managing the relationship. At the very least it will give you an opportunity to repeat what you want from them and for them to feel their views are being heard. At best it may give you a clearer view of what they want from the relationship and suggest possible room for manoeuvre. Start to manage them differently and, who knows, it may encourage a more positive result.

Part of sustaining any healthy relationship means finding things in the other person you admire and want to encourage. It is worth remembering that when we say we dislike someone we don't dislike all of them, just bits of them. Rather than focusing on the negative behaviours, reverse the self-fulfilling prophesy of criticism and negative reaction by concentrating on the good parts. Catch them doing things approximately right rather than waiting for them to do them perfectly. Make a point of praising what they do well, preferably in front of others or in writing. Not only does thinking and talking about the good in others change the way they relate to us, it often helps to change our perception of them as people.

Finally, as a way of repairing a troublesome relationship, consider getting help from others who may have found a better way of dealing with that person. What sometimes makes the process of dealing with problem staff even more problematic is that when our best efforts fail we are inclined to become defensive and over-react, which only adds to the problem. Yet many of those difficult people at some time probably worked for a boss who brought out the best in them and it may have been that he or she knew which buttons to press. Although you may not discover a very different approach you may get some ideas from others on how to draw them closer and in doing so find them more willing to respond.

CHANGE THE JOB OR SITUATION

While it may not be the first or the final strategy in dealing with poor performers, at the end of the day you may have to consider a more direct approach to changing either the job or the person.

As with any relationship they often get into difficulty because the needs of one or both parties are not being met. Needs theories in motivation suggest that most people come to work with expectations, and if they are not fulfilled it can affect their performance and behaviour. While needs are satisfied for some staff through tangible things like money, fringe benefits or close interpersonal relationships, for others they are mainly internal to the job itself in the form of interesting work, challenging assignments or opportunities for personal development. And though it is easy to conclude that if other staff are satisfied with their lot then so should the problem person, it is clear that individuals have different needs and some are able to satisfy those needs outside work in a variety of social activities, sports or family.

If one of your staff is under-performing or has become difficult, consider whether their needs are being met in the job and make some attempt to find out what they want. While you may not be able to satisfy them directly you may be able to help them find other challenges or experiences that will give them more of a sense of achievement, growth or fun. According to Maltz[1] a great deal of the failure experienced by students is down to the fact that they were not given assignments early on at which they could succeed, while at a more general level it is a truism that people who produce good results usually feel good about themselves.

Also consider that for some staff the job may have become routine or less challenging and they are simply reacting in ways that people do when they are bored, even to the point where they sabotage things to make life more interesting. However, as one survey of over 200 workers found, not all staff are bored by the same tasks, especially if there are opportunities for compensating activities such as being part of a well-functioning team, meeting the public or having occasional opportunities for travel. It cites six major reasons for boredom: repetitiveness, job constraints, frequent interruptions, lack of challenge, an unclear job and the never-ending nature of the work.

If the work being done by your problem staff is mainly routine or repetitive consider building more planning and control into their jobs. Even with fairly basic tasks there are ways of involving people in their own quality control, troubleshooting or customer contacts. If none of those is an option, consider giving them more control of things that are not directly related to the job, such as flexi-time arrangements, deciding what times of the day to tackle certain tasks and allowing them to rotate boring work or do it in a social setting rather than individually. A best-selling business book, *Fish!*, explores the phenomenon of the Pike Place Fish Market in Seattle where a routine and fairly unpleasant environment has transformed itself into a highly motivated and entertaining spectacle by focusing on four basic principles:[2]

1. Letting the staff choose their own attitude – by inspiring staff to determine their individual philosophy and challenges in the job.
2. Encouraging play – on the basis that fun leads to creativity and vice versa, inviting staff to be innovative through competitions,

brainstorming, special assignments, rotation and improvement groups.
3. Making the customer's day – encouraging staff to focus on the client's needs, finding ways to surprise and delight them and making those contacts memorable.
4. Being present with the staff – engaging people in creating the atmosphere. Being available to them and fostering the conditions in which they can build relationships with each other.

One assumption frequently held by many managers is that workers in low-level jobs are less responsible and need to be closely supervised. This view often adds to feelings of frustration by those staff and fuels a self-fulfilling prophecy of poor motivation and close supervision. Reversing the tendency to treat workers in low-level jobs differently may involve finding ways to praise them for work well done, setting clear standards, agreeing goals and publicly tracking performance so they begin to see themselves as winners and their contribution as important to the overall effort. A survey carried out with clients of a travel company which runs hostels for overseas students found the room cleaners were a critical group in terms of their contribution to customer service because they were in a position to deal with minor problems, interact with the guests and source key information for the hostel. The acknowledgement of their role had a major effect on the way they were seen by the rest of the organisation and on their self-esteem. Paying more positive regard to staff in lower-level jobs may require more frequent job reviews, encouraging them to set individual or group goals and getting their ideas for improving quality and service. Above all it is important not to assume that apparently low-level and routine jobs can't be made more motivating and less problematic by tailoring them to the requirements of the individual and the work group.

WHEN TO START THE FUNERAL

Sometimes, however, none of the above strategies work and it is time to modify or terminate the relationship. But as Jack Welch advises, there should be no surprises. Individuals should know well in advance what they have to do to avoid more serious consequences and given adequate opportunity to reform. If there is a need for more drastic action start by documenting the evidence, the efforts you have made to resolve the problem and the person's responses before engaging in a more formal disciplinary or dismissals process.

One longer-term option is to put some distance between yourself and the problem person. It may be possible to transfer them to another department or a new manager where the accumulated mistrust can be avoided. Alternatively, refer them to a third party in HR or an outside counsellor where they may be more open to accepting help. Apart from coming to the situation with some fresh thinking a third party may also help you listen to each other. However, if none of the above works then start the dismissals process conscious that it is a last resort and may not be an easy option. Unless you have clearly documented the situation and they have no grounds for claiming harassment or unfair dismissal it may be difficult to get them to leave without reaction from other staff or inviting quasi-legal action.

Difficult staff and poor performers can take up a great deal of management time, become a major cause of stress and have negative effects on the rest of the team. And the sympathies of the team may not be entirely with the manager as difficult staff often work hard to gain sympathy from their colleagues. But in dealing with problem staff it is important to remember that most people want to do a good day's work and very few people are deliberately difficult. Rather than giving way to the more common reactions to problem staff, such as avoiding them or controlling their behaviour, explore whether there is an obvious cause and try to resolve the issue. Alternatively, confront their behaviour or find better ways to cope with the effects. If those strategies are unsuccessful then look for ways to change the situation or the person.

In adopting any of the strategies outlined also put yourself in the shoes of the problem person and try to see things from their perspective. They may not understand why they are underperforming or difficult and there are no easy solutions for them either. If one of the rooms in your house catches fire it is fairly clear what you have to do, but if you don't like your job or the people you are working with it is a much more complex and confusing situation. Rather than accepting staff retiring on the job or putting their energies into trouble-making, consider it part of the management challenge to make your people into winners, which is what most of them aspire to become.

CHAPTER 8

Making Delegation Happen

Ask any group of managers whether they are working under pressure and the majority will answer 'yes'. Ask the same people to imagine their boss offering them an all expenses paid trip to a conference in the Far East if they can find the time to attend and, without hesitation, the response is an equally unequivocal 'yes'. It is a minor miracle that managers who claim they are working under pressure can always find time for the things they really want to do, whether a golf outing, an interesting seminar or an overseas business trip.

Yet, examine the amount of time that most managers give to coaching their staff, to counselling poor performers, managing by wandering around or doing mini job reviews and it adds up to surprisingly little. The explanation generally on offer is they would willingly give more quality time to staff were it not for the many routine and urgent demands of the job. Like other management functions delegation often gets sidetracked to the more immediate concerns of the day because managers are required to balance two competing types of work.

On the one hand, managers spend a significant part of their day on routine and reactive tasks such as attending meetings, dealing with minor crises, sorting out problems and handling interruptions, which typically get done either because they are institutionalised commitments like the Monday morning meeting or because they demand an immediate response. On the other hand, managers also have to find time for the more proactive tasks in the job which, although important, are often less immediate or demanding because improving communications, developing staff or reviewing workloads are less tangible, and the results are only seen in the longer-term.

As such, the proactive side of the manager's job tends to be less attractive than the reactive things that can be dispatched in minutes. So, while they may complain about the amount of routine and urgency in their day, not only do those things get done, but managers are attracted to the immediacy of the telephone, the e-mail and the unexpected drop-in. While it is not uncommon for a manager with twenty minutes to spare before a meeting to make a few phone calls or reply to a couple of e-mails it is less likely they would consider using those same precious minutes to check on the status of the training plan or coach one of their staff who is having problems on a project.

An added consequence of the daily work pressure is that managers can end up spending a significant amount of time on queries and problems from staff at the expense of more important issues such as coaching, monitoring progress and recognising individuals for their efforts. And while there may be valid reasons for not giving sufficient quality time to staff, it is a truism that most things get done if you make time for them. You pass exams if you make time for study, you get fit if you make time for exercise and you develop trusting relationships by making time for your staff. Conversely, if you regard your staff as a priority and are not giving them time then, by definition, they are not a priority and they will soon recognise by your actions that you don't value them or their contribution.

SCHEDULE TIME FOR LETTING GO

Analysis of time accounting exercises clearly show that while most managers could give some of their work to others, what gets

Making Delegation Happen

in the way is that it is often easier and quicker to do it themselves. And while it is a common belief that shedding the more onerous and time-consuming things in the job would make more time available for staff it is based on a false premise that letting go of some things is a guarantee of giving more time to others. In reality it may simply mean that one set of urgency and routine is replaced with another. The way to start making time for real delegation is not by looking for ways to let go of things but recognising it as a key part of the job and finding ways to make it happen.

Three practical ways of finding quality time for delegation include firstly making space in the day and week for your longer-term goals on the basis that the more committed you are to the things you want to achieve the easier it is to let go. Secondly, more quality time for staff can be made available by scheduling for things that will only happen if they are firm commitments in your Diary, such as carrying out mini reviews, having team meetings and coaching poor performers. And thirdly, it often helps to convert aspirations into reality if they are institutionalised as commitments in the day, week or month as a way of ensuring they get done.

KEEP APPOINTMENTS WITH YOURSELF

As suggested in Chapter 2, the place to start with delegation is not what you want to give away but what you want to hang onto, which for managers includes the longer-term challenges in the job. A couple of simple disciplines for ensuring you are giving the right kind of time to the things you want to achieve for the longer-term include making a routine of setting and working to priorities and using your Diary to make them happen.

While it helps to have longer-term objectives for your area, as signposts to the future and for encouraging others to share the journey, they are often too far into the future to provide any immediate focus, and the tendency is to leave them until the threat of a

133

review approaches. One way of combating the tendency to procrastinate on major challenges is to set milestones along the way in the form of a monthly wish list of things you could do in the next few months to drive your longer-term ambitions in the shorter term.

It makes sense on one day each month to take ten minutes to draw up a list of all the things you want to achieve or at least get some mileage on in the next few months, and select two or three as priorities. Let the others go, reminding yourself that trying to focus on too many things usually leads to focusing on nothing. Also, be mindful that most people's energy is for what has to be done today or this week. So, while it is important to have monthly priorities, the way to action them is by identifying simple tasks to drive them in the next few weeks and selecting a couple you could deliver on almost immediately (see Table 8.1)

In drawing up a list of short-term tasks for each priority it is important to recognise there is no logical sequence to achieving most things in this life, whether finding a partner, passing an exam or losing weight. The key to making things happen is to break them into small bite-sized chunks and start on the easy ones as a way of getting some early success and energy to go on to the next step. And, as a way of recognising your progress on the longer-term

Table 8.1: Fuelling Priorities with Tasks

1. Priority (2–3 months) – Complete 10 Staff Reviews
2. Short Term Tasks (1–2 weeks)

    a) Check last year's Personal Development Plans*
    b) Draw up a list of possible goals for each staff member
    c) Arrange four interviews*
    d) Do a plan for carrying out the reviews
    e) Revisit my own objectives for the year*

* The three tasks that would provide immediate success

Making Delegation Happen

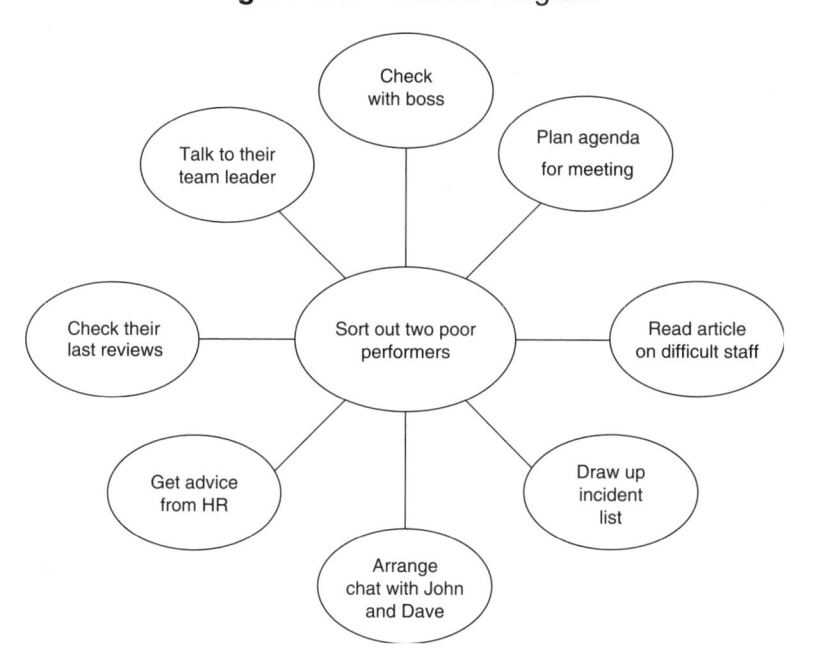

Figure 8.1: Bubble Diagram

- Check with boss
- Plan agenda for meeting
- Talk to their team leader
- Check their last reviews
- Sort out two poor performers
- Read article on difficult staff
- Get advice from HR
- Draw up incident list
- Arrange chat with John and Dave

priorities consider doing them up as bubble charts and having them on the wall in front of your desk so that as you complete each short-term task you get the pleasure of crossing them off with a highlighter pen (Figure 8.1). Finally, use your Diary to block out time for some tasks, making them into commitments in the same way you would meetings or appointments.[1]

In addition to ensuring your Diary reflects priorities for the future, also consider blocking out some time for planning. Several surveys of what managers feel they should be giving more time to in their day identify thinking and planning as top of the list. Yet they are also the very things that tend to go by the board when managers are under pressure. Consequently planning is often done in a rush when things become urgent or is tackled outside working hours when managers have least energy. One way of committing to the less tangible and future-focused tasks like planning and thinking is to allocate chunks of time to them. Consider blocking out two separate hours a week in your Diary for activities such as catching up on a backlog of reading, working on key projects, reviewing your staff development plans or having review meetings with your key people.

INSTITUTIONALISE CONTACTS WITH YOUR STAFF

While managers may spend a great deal of time with their staff, in some cases as much as 50–60 per cent of the day, much of it is taken up dealing with queries and resolving problems. There is a significant difference between the kind of time that managers spend dealing with routine staff queries and the amount of time they invest in developing working relationships. And, unless your commitment to supporting staff in taking ownership of their responsibilities is scheduled for it will inevitably give way to the more immediate demands in the day. A few simple ways of ensuring sufficient quality time for your staff include scheduling to touch base with people (MBWA), having regular one-on-ones, periodically clarifying roles and tasks, and institutionalising goal-setting and review sessions.

MBWA

With its origins in Hewlett Packard, and popularised by the book *In Search of Excellence*,[2] the principle of managing by wandering around has been further legitimised by a move away from hands-on management styles to more benign ways of touching base with staff. Letting go of real responsibility means developing less invasive ways of following up on delegated tasks so that you don't unconsciously take back what you give away. Whether through regular weekly meetings, daily briefings, review sessions or using your Diary to block out time in the week to chat with individuals over coffee, those things are often best scheduled as mutual commitments to manage and be managed. And while it makes sense for managers to commit time to MBWA it may also be important to Diary it on a regular basis, particularly if you have become somewhat detached from your staff through long hours at meetings or their busy workloads.

> *A series of research interviews were carried out in a large semi-state organisation that was going through a major transition. A new CEO had been appointed who made it his business to visit every manager in the organisation, soliciting their views on the changes and discussing the implications for each area. At one of the research interviews a manager began to relate, with tears welling in his eyes, how the new CEO had visited him in his office to solicit his views and let him know how much he and the company valued his contribution. The emotion in his voice stemmed from the fact that it was the first time in twenty years of service that a senior manager had made any effort to visit him in his office or to acknowledge his efforts, and it was obvious how much it meant to him. Surely many other staff have similar experiences of a boss who rarely comes near them unless there is a problem or a favour they need.*

Frequent One-on-Ones

Some years ago, on study leave in the United States, I worked in two companies, one a microprocessor plant and the other a telephone utility. On one of my visits home a friend asked if there were any real differences between the American management style and our own. I thought for a moment before commenting that in many respects the approaches were very similar except that in both companies even the most junior of managers made time to sit down with each staff member on a monthly basis to find out how things were going and give them feedback.

Whether it was culturally specific to those two organisations or a more general style of managing I never discovered, but there is a tendency for managers to wait for the obligatory annual review to be open and honest with their staff. And while many organisations have introduced elements of performance management, there is still a reluctance by some managers to do more than the minimum of relationship building with their staff, even though a wealth of evidence suggests they do want feedback and an opportunity to discuss the work. Although there may be little choice for managers in carrying out annual reviews, it also makes sense to block out an hour or two each week for mini-reviews or for casual chats with staff. Not only are those contacts useful as information exchanges, but they also provide an opportunity to repeat expectations and remind your staff how much you value their efforts.

Role and Task Reviews

As well as making time to review individual performance in the job it may also be important now and again to remind your staff why they are doing what they are doing. In the present climate where many people are working under pressure it is easy to lose sight of their expected contribution to the department or unit – and as Thomas Carlyle once suggested, 'nothing is so terrible as activity without insight'. While most organisations today are trying to get more done with less people we are also witnessing increasing numbers of staff putting in long hours and feeling stressed and undervalued. If that is a reflection of your area it may be worth inviting your staff to renew their focus or review how well they are spending their time.

On the basis that most people end up busy, the real issue is 'busy doing what?' Are some of your staff less than focused on

Making Delegation Happen

their priorities? Do you have staff who are capable of taking more responsibility but you fear over-loading them? Are some of your people busy but with little reference to what you are trying to achieve? Have some individuals carved out a comfortable niche for themselves and erected barriers to taking on other work? It may be useful now and again to get your staff to examine their role, the time they spend on job-related activities and their function in assisting in what you are trying to achieve.

> *According to Dr Thom Baguely of Nottingham Trent University, and reported by the Automobile Association, 'driving dunces' waste 2.3 billion miles each year by taking the same route every day to work. They suffer from what is termed the 'set effect', meaning that once they find a route they tend to stick to it even though it is not the quickest or the cheapest. According to the research it can take up to a year for them to realise that there is another route that could save them time and petrol. In a similar way the set effect applies to staff who get into a routine that may not be the most efficient way to do the job or get the results they are trying to achieve.*

One method for encouraging staff to reflect on their function is to have an annual Role Review. While the exercise provides an opportunity for dialogue the focus should be on their work functions rather than on the detail of the job. Some questions that will prompt individuals to confront issues in relation to their role include:

- How do you see your function/your contribution to the department?
- What do you think your boss (me) is demanding from you?
- What do you consider as key tasks in your job?

- In what ways has your role changed in the past year?
- How do you see it changing/would you like to see it change in the next six months?
- What is confusing or unclear about your role?
- How do others sometimes view your function that is different from how you see it?
- Ideally what would you like your job to be?
- How would you describe your role in one sentence?
- What additional support do you need from your colleagues in carrying out your functions?

When carrying out a Role Review, allow at least fifteen minutes to ask open questions, keeping notes as you go along and summarising now and again what you think you are hearing. Also, challenge any vagueness in their responses. When quizzed about their role many people retreat into vague language that includes words like 'to coordinate', 'liaise with' or 'monitor', which disguises an uncertainty or ambiguity about their function. At the end of the session summarise what came across, particularly where there are differences in perception. And while there may be some advantage in writing up a Role Profile for each person more important is to document what you agreed, including how you see their role changing for the future, and feed that information into the goal-setting process.

> A useful exercise for clarifying role confusion and work boundaries is Role Negotiation, a tough approach to job clarification. It involves the manager having a one-on-one with each member of staff, or alternatively doing the exercise with the group. In preparation for the exercise each person writes down on separate pieces of paper all the things they would like each other individual to do more of and less of, and the things they want them to continue doing in their job. Either by putting each person in focus at a time for ten to fifteen minutes

Making Delegation Happen

or simply exchanging the pieces of paper each person agrees to change their role and behaviour in return for changes on the part of other individuals. At the end of the exercise each person states what they are going to do for the future and those commitments are reviewed at a later date by the group or manager. The benefit of doing it as a group exercise is it reminds each person that their role affects and is affected by each other individual in the group. The more they understand each other's role and their dependency on each other the more likely individuals are to appreciate the contribution of their colleagues and the more likely they are to assist others in doing their jobs.

An alternative way of encouraging staff to reflect on what they are doing is an annual or bi-annual time accounting exercise. The process is best started by sharing a view that everyone, including you, runs the risk of being busy on the wrong things at the expense of the things that should be given more time. Also, suggest that an annual time log can be a useful tool for self-analysis and the data is mainly for their benefit.

> *As Peter Drucker confirms in his management writings, there is a fundamental confusion between effectiveness and efficiency that stands between doing the right things and doing things right. 'There is surely nothing quite so useless as doing with great efficiency what should not be done at all'.*

Keeping a time log involves each individual recording what they do, quarter of an hour by quarter of an hour, over a couple of typical working days. That exercise is usually followed by an individual or team meeting to share the data, discuss the outcome and get feedback from their colleagues (for more detail on the analysis refer to Chapter 3). Inviting your staff individually or as a group to keep a time log now and again can be a useful exercise, particularly if they have expressed concerns about unequal workloads, long hours, time pressures or being less than satisfied with their achievements. And, as much as possible, encourage them to reach their own conclusions and to suggest ways in which they could be more effective for the future.

Regular Goal-Setting and Review

While the increasing use of formal performance reviews reflects a growing need, especially in high labour cost organisations, to increase individual and team productivity, it is also an attempt to encourage open dialogue between bosses and their staff. In many organisations today reviews are done more frequently than annually, sometimes even quarterly, and usually relate to goals that have been set in the previous period.

As a way of encouraging staff to be more thoughtful and focused, one common output of the job review process is a Personal Development Plan (PDP) together with an agreed set of measurable goals for the following period. Whatever form the job review takes, the important issue is that managers and staff have ownership of the process and the focus is on dialogue and agreement rather than evaluation and criticism.

Any goal-setting and review process should be seen as part of managing the relationship between the manager and their staff. Managers do need to know their people are being stretched rather than settling into a comfortable niche, and staff need to be reminded periodically that no one is being asked to do just the same as yesterday. In addition to keeping staff focused on their longer-term challenges, goal-setting and review is also an important way of building responsibility for delegation into the manager's role. The process, which usually includes a review of each individual's performance and an agreement on future action, means that managers have to clarify their expectations, encourage

Making Delegation Happen

staff to take ownership of their performance, monitor progress and reward performance.

Whether it forms part of a formal or an informal process, critical to making job reviews work are some of the following ground rules:

1. Have a clear purpose in mind – remind your staff why you are doing the review and what they can hope to get from participating. Express your commitment to the process and have a few clear messages you want to get across to each individual.
2. Be prepared – prior to the review, assess how well you think the person has performed in the previous period and identify a couple of challenges for the next period. Also have one or two pieces of feedback to give them, at least one of which should be positive.
3. Agree a time and place – reviews are best carried out in a relaxed atmosphere such as a meeting room or a quiet space in the canteen. Also agree a realistic timescale, which should be generous. You aren't going to get a meaningful review, including agreement on new goals, completed in fifteen minutes.
4. Have a simple agenda for the meeting – but more importantly take time to share views about their past performance and challenges for the future.
5. Keep the dialogue informal – if there is a standard form try to get through it reasonably quickly and put it to one side in favour of a more open exchange of views. At the end of the review summarise what has been agreed and suggest a deadline for getting back to them with a written synopsis and agreed goals.

Staff appraisal has attracted a bad press over the years, mainly because of delays in carrying them out, lack of ownership by managers, a focus on evaluation and poor follow-up on the actions agreed. But, at least it ensures that once or twice a year there is a commitment to sitting down with each member of staff to share views and identify future challenges in the job. And, unless goal-setting is established as part of a regular commitment to delegation, the fallback is likely to be into the comfort zone of 'busyness' by staff and an unwillingness by managers to share the important challenges in their own jobs.

PRACTICAL TOOLS FOR DELEGATION

Most important things get done if you give them time, and one of the best approaches to making time for delegation is scheduling it in the same way you would appointments, meetings or other commitments. Several simple ways of scheduling for delegation include using a To Do List, Weekly Planner, Delegation Checklist and Training Plan.

To Do List (TDL)

As a way of making time in the day for the important things, a To Do List is useful both for identifying where you want to focus yourself and for encouraging your staff to work to their priorities. While many people keep lists of things they are trying to get done few use them to manage themselves or encourage others to manage their time. And by themselves simple lists are a killer in the sense that they get longer and longer and the temptation is to do the easy tasks first on the basis that I will get those done and then get into the more important jobs. Unfortunately it doesn't work that way as more and more small things get in the way of the important stuff. Though it starts life as a simple list of tasks for the day, what makes the TDL into an important tool for self-management and for delegation is the activities are prioritised as A, B, C and D.

- A's are important things you want to get done today
- B's are potential A's, once you get the A's done

Making Delegation Happen

- C's are things you don't want to forget but are less important
- D's are things you want to delegate to others

The key to managing a To Do List is having no more than three A's as priorities and getting into them as early in the day as possible. All too often it is the easy things that get done first and the important things are left until times of the day when people have least energy. As you get the A's done simply re-prioritise some of the B's into A's so that as you go through the day you are always focusing on the most important tasks first. Also, make a habit of delegating the D's early in the day so that your staff can add them to their TDL and schedule them into their day.

While the TDL is an effective way of ensuring that you focus on the important tasks in your day it is also a simple device for encouraging staff to work to priorities rather than getting sidetracked by urgency and routine, and for integrating what they are doing with what you are trying to achieve.

At the end of a time management seminar with the supervisors and department managers of a supermarket chain a review session was held to discuss how the participants could best use what they had learned. One suggestion taken up by the group was that the Section Supervisors would check first thing in the morning with their department managers to see if they wanted them to put anything on their To Do List and in turn let their bosses know what they saw as their priorities for the day. It was also agreed that they would share their experiences of keeping a TDL at the weekly management meeting. Not only did it help to facilitate a more open dialogue between supervisors and managers in terms of their different responsibilities, it also encouraged department managers to start involving supervisors in the longer-term priorities for the department.

Weekly Planner

While the TDL is useful for ensuring that managers focus on the important things and their staff keep in touch with daily priorities, there may also be some benefit in having a weekly plan to share some of the longer-term tasks. Completing a Weekly Planner consists of taking five minutes on a Monday morning to draw up a list of all the things you want to get done that week and making sure that some of them contribute to what you are trying to achieve for the longer-term.

From the list identify three or four as priorities and spend a few minutes breaking each one into smaller bite-sized tasks. In similar fashion to the TDL, prioritise those tasks as A's, B's, C's and D's. Get into the A's as early as possible on Monday, and as you get those things done upgrade the B's and C's into A's so that you are always working on three A's. And one small tip before deciding the priority for a particular task is to ask 'why me?' And if there is no good reason why that task should be done by you then consider assigning it as a D. When tasks are completed or assigned to others get the pleasure of crossing them off the list as a check on what has been done and what is yet to be achieved for that week to be effective.

> *Organising on a weekly basis provides much greater balance and context than daily planning. There seems to be implicit cultural recognition of the week as a single, complete unit of time. Business, education, and many other facets of society operate within the framework of the week, designating certain days for focused investment and others for relaxation and inspiration* – Stephen Covey, *The Seven Habits of Highly Effective People.*

Not only is the Weekly Planner a good way of helping managers to focus on the important things in their week but it is also a simple

Making Delegation Happen

way of sharing responsibility for longer-term tasks with their staff. As a variation, consider doing a Weekly Planner for the whole department, assigning tasks to specific individuals and keeping the list in a public place so they can see what has been done and what has yet to be completed. Better still, involve them in creating the Weekly Planner or set up a small group to take responsibility for monitoring its progress.

Delegation Checklist

Another way of keeping track of tasks you want to let go to others is using a Delegation Checklist (see Table 8.2). How often have you given jobs to your staff only to forget whether you had allocated them, how long ago and when they promised to have them completed? One simple way of ensuring that you don't lose touch with tasks you give away to others is to record and monitor them.

As tasks arise that can be delegated, simply jot them down on a list and, as the opportunity presents itself, delegate them, noting the initials of the person and the date they were allocated. For tasks that aren't so urgent, or where completion

Table 8.2: Delegation Checklist

Name	Allocated	Task	Due Date
C	20/08	Type up climate survey	30/09
C	20/08	Get four copies of workbook	
C	20/08	Invoice GRS	22/09
L	26/09	Send fax to Marit	
C	20/08	Get "Values" article	
P	25/08	Regional meeting agenda	
AV	29/09	Make labels for files	
C	01/10	Get proofs from Claire	
C	03/10	Prepare notes for Wexford	09/10

is required by a specific deadline, agree a Due Date, as much as possible getting the individual to suggest a realistic timescale. Note the due dates in your diary with a reminder to monitor progress some time before the due date. As tasks are completed get the pleasure of crossing them off the list and at a glance you can see what has been done and what you may need to chase up.

Training Plan

While letting go of responsibility to your staff makes eminent sense, it does assume they have the ability to take on the new tasks to which they have been assigned. Although personal development plans (PDPs) can provide an important link between training needs and individual development it may also help if you map the overall requirements for your unit on an annual or bi-annual training plan.

A simple training plan for a team or department consists of listing all the tasks carried out by that section (or the knowledge and skills required) across the top of a simple grid chart and the names of individuals in the team down the left hand side. On the resulting grid it is then easy to make decisions about who has the ability to carry out each task, identify performance weaknesses, assess the required capacities on each job, allowing for sickness and holidays, and plan for suitable training.

The final outcome is to agree development plans with each individual and to source suitable training. And apart from formal training do not ignore the informal methods by which staff gain much of their confidence in the job. Some of the most important career development experiences reported by staff are not formal training opportunities but less organised events along the way, such as being assigned to a project team, having to make a presentation, being put in charge of a task group or being asked to troubleshoot a difficult situation.

Making Delegation Happen

Although staff training is an important aspect of the delegation process that frequently gets overlooked unless it is scheduled, other elements are best managed by regularising them for particular times of the week or month, such as coaching sessions, mini-reviews or team meetings. And while some events only happen if managers commit time to them, others can be a useful vehicle for involving your staff in making them a reality. Consider involving people in their own development by assigning them to customer service teams, nominating them for a group to oversee the annual climate survey, or get key staff to take responsibility for monitoring the training plan, instruct new hires or source training opportunities.

The key to achieving most important things in life is firstly committing to them and then finding time to make them happen. In the same spirit that Yogi Bearra once commented 'you can observe a lot by just watching', so it is true that 'you can achieve a lot of things by just scheduling for them'. Real delegation only happens if you make time for it to happen.

CHAPTER 9

What Real Delegators Do

While it is sometimes viewed simplistically as a set of skills, procedures and processes, one way of getting to the core of real delegation is examining the influences and effects that good bosses have on their staff. What are the qualities of a 'best boss' and are there specific behaviours that make them stand out in the eyes of those who work for them? What sets them apart from other managers and how do they inspire their staff to raise their game?

Most people recognise and value a good or even a great boss at some stage in their working lives, who brought out the best in them and in many cases left a legacy to follow. And though we may acknowledge the contribution of a good boss we can also learn from having a difficult or intolerable boss, who in other ways may contribute to our development, or at least provide lessons we will never choose to repeat. In a recent survey over one third of workers described the relationship with their boss as 'almost unbearable', while another third were less than satisfied with them. On the other hand 15 per cent said they had an excellent relationship and 21 per cent said it was pretty good. In the survey of over 350 people 86 per cent identified having a good manager as critical in terms of letting them get on with the job, trusting them to use their initiative and being available for support and guidance when needed.[1]

As with great leaders and successful teams what we initially see in a good boss are the qualities that attract us to them as mentors, coaches, role models or friends. And, in the same way that some leaders are invested with attributes after the event because they were successful, if those people had failed they may not have been seen in quite the same light. Would Churchill or Montgomery have been seen as great leaders if they had failed to win the war and would Jack Welch or Richard Branson have been fêted as entrepreneurs and managers if their businesses had not succeeded? Nonetheless, examining the qualities of good bosses is one place to start identifying the differences between those who may have been successful on the backs of their staff and others who mastered the ability to work with and through people.

The findings from a recent survey, carried out by the author, of over 120 employees from a variety of organisations suggest the main qualities of a best boss as their willingness to trust people, having a clear sense of purpose, being open to new ideas and as being great motivators of their staff. But while such sobriquets shed some light on their attributes, more revealing are the behaviours that contributed to their staff ascribing them with such qualities. From a list of behaviours associated with the qualities of a best boss the top seven emerge as follows:

Best bosses…
1. Make quality time for their staff
2. Have a genuine interest and concern for people
3. Are demanding – push their people hard
4. Solicit and volunteer positive and negative feedback
5. Use predominantly hands-off styles
6. Show positive regard and respect for staff
7. Press the right buttons to get the best from people

What Real Delegators Do

QUALITY TIME FOR STAFF

The findings of this survey suggest that the most consistent behaviour of best bosses is they make time for their staff in a number of different ways, from being available to an openness to new ideas and suggestions, and most of all listening to them. And while listening includes the way they handle formal situations such as team meetings and job reviews, it also involves them making space for less structured contacts, such as having a genuine open-door policy, touching base frequently with their staff, taking time to listen and never making people feel they are wasting their time.

> *A study on how well managers listen to their staff produced some interesting results. 114 managers from the hospitality industry were asked to rate their listening abilities while six staff for each manager were also asked to rate their boss's listening skills.*
>
> *Analysis of the bottom 25 per cent of managers (those who were given a score of 4.3 or less out of 7 by their staff) found that 94 per cent had rated themselves close to the top of the scale as good or very good listeners. The researchers concluded that the main reason it is so hard to improve the communications skills of managers is that very few think they have a problem.*[2]

While being available means just that in some cases, in others it is much more about the quality of those contacts. For some staff it is their boss's willingness to listen without evaluating their ideas or giving advice, but rather helping them to tease things out for themselves, prompting them to find solutions and keeping ownership with them. For others it includes a boss being open to new ideas even if they are at odds with their own views, and encouraging and supporting staff in implementing their proposals.

GENUINE INTEREST AND CONCERN

Not only are best bosses viewed as encouraging their staff in general ways through making time to listen, they are also seen as having a genuine interest in their development, through coaching them on immediate issues and showing practical concern for their career aspirations. Many in the survey commented on their boss having a real interest in their career even if it meant losing them to another department, and that encouragement went a long way to improving their self-esteem. Also contributing to an increased confidence in their own abilities were many comments about a best boss being willing to give them early responsibility and trusting them even when they lacked experience or were new to a task.

> 'At every opportunity she puts challenging projects my way and gives me full rein to customise them to my skill set.'

> 'He always pushes me to come up with solutions and gives me space to implement them, even at the risk of making mistakes.'

Not only are the development opportunities provided by a best boss a way of encouraging their staff but those opportunities are rarely given without support. In many cases best bosses are seen to help their staff take on extra responsibilities through mentoring and follow-up to ensure they are being stretched but not beyond the bounds of their ability. Interest and support also extends to helping individuals resolve issues that may be preventing them from making progress on a task or project, whether the blocks are political, staffing or resourcing issues.

> 'While I was involved in dealing with a difficult member of staff, who was claiming harassment, my boss informed HR that I had his total support and he would ensure that there were no negative repercussions from the episode.'

CLEAR DEMANDS AND TOUGH EMPATHY

While some respondents identify them as tough and demanding, in many cases they also recognise a best boss as getting more out of them than they ever thought possible. And while they value having a boss with a clear and challenging vision for the area, more important it seems is that he or she communicates what they expect in the form of a clear role and goals, agreed deliverables and regular reviews, as a way of promoting internal self-management rather than external control of their performance.

> 'He was firm but fair – you knew exactly where you stood with him and exactly what he expected from you.'

> 'She knows exactly what she needs from the team, delegates the work appropriately and makes people responsible and definitely part of the team.'

Unlike traditional human relations approaches to people management real delegators appear to practice 'tough empathy', giving staff what they need rather than what they want and pushing them to be the best they can be. 'Grow or go', is the motto of organisations and managers who subscribe to this view.[3] Good people managers, it is suggested, provide an equal balance between respect for the individual and focus on the task, implying that most staff want a boss who not only cares passionately about them but equally is concerned about their contribution. From the survey it appears that many staff value a boss who makes clear demands on them and touches base regularly, not only to listen but to push them for progress, while at the same time coaching them towards the desired results.

> 'The goals were made clear to me. I always knew where I was required to go in the long- and the short-term. His feedback was always useful and the reviews frequent.'

CORRECTIVE AND ENCOURAGING FEEDBACK

That the boss is up front in terms of giving feedback and inviting response is, in the eyes of many staff, an important indicator of a trusting relationship, as long as it is complemented by a willingness to listen and support them.

> 'He told me that I had done a terrible interview, but offered to help me plan for the next opportunity. He did and I was successful.'

> 'If you are doing a good job you know it, and if you are doing a bad job you also know.'

It appears that many employees make little distinction between positive and negative feedback when it comes to a respected boss, viewing both as constructive if they are given fairly and in the right spirit. In this regard best bosses are little different from others with whom we have close relationships. Central to building a trusting relationship is a willingness to be open in giving and inviting feedback – it is the way in which we deepen our relationships and significantly through lack of openness that they break down. Good bosses, intuitively or through a learned process, recognise the importance of feedback in moulding their staff and understand that it needs to be continuous rather than periodic. In the same way that children need frequent praise and encouragement in all aspects of their development so, as the book *The One Minute Manager* proclaims, 'feedback is the breakfast of champions'.[4]

MAINLY HANDS-OFF STYLES

In describing their best boss as being more 'hands-off' than hands-on, typical behaviours range from not standing over people but allowing them to get on with things, to trusting them implicitly to use their initiative. Rather than been seen as laissez-faire, hands-off styles are viewed in combination with frequent informal or formal contacts that include the boss regularly touching base, having an open-door policy, being available and providing them with honest feedback.

The more participative and open styles exercised by best bosses in the survey were viewed by many as a sign that, although demanding, they were prepared to let go of the detail. And, in terms of the amount of control they exercise in the relationship, best bosses are seen as allowing their staff considerable latitude in the way they manage themselves. As long as the work gets done and the bases are covered they trust people to be honest and fair in managing their own workloads and time.

> 'He allowed me to manage the department my way and that included managing my own hours and holidays.'

> 'He doesn't stand over you but allows you to use your own initiative while being there if you need guidance.'

POSITIVE REGARD AND RESPECT

While they may sometimes be seen as tough and uncompromising, best bosses are more likely to recognise the contribution of their staff in a variety of ways, from recommending them to others to defending them when required and publicly appreciating their efforts. Some memorable incidents reported by survey respondents include being brought into meetings with key clients, being asked to make presentations to senior management, impromptu celebrations on passing exams, and being praised in front of their peers when targeted results or tight deadlines were met.

Some survey respondents also highlighted the fact that their boss did not claim praise for themselves when it may have been the easy option, but used it as an opportunity to get recognition for their staff. Many also recognised incidents where their boss came to their defence when they were being blocked, harassed or unfairly treated by others. Other positive incidents related to personal acts of kindness, such as a boss telephoning them every day when their father was dying, treating the unit to a meal after a demanding month and dealing with the staff and their families in thoughtful and caring ways.

> 'He felt I was being underpaid by the company and through helping me with suggestions and ideas I managed to get a significant pay rise.'

> 'I set up a new system to track information on securities. He said it was a great idea, encouraged me to implement it and then recognised me at a meeting with his boss for the great work I had done.'

PRESSING THE RIGHT BUTTONS

Although best bosses are characterised by specific behaviours in the survey, knowing how to manage the relationship in terms of pushing the right buttons appears to be the overarching skill. A recent survey by the Gallup Organisation of over 80,000 managers concludes that the one attribute which sets great managers apart is they discover what is unique about each individual and capitalise on it. According to an article 'What Great Managers Do',[5] based in part on the Gallop survey, it is exactly the opposite of what great leaders do, which is to create a vision of a better place and rally people towards that future. In contrast the job of the manager, the article proposes, is to discover what is unique about each individual and turn those talents into superior performance. And while there is no suggestion that great leaders can't also be great managers, to excel at both they have to be aware of the different skills required by each role.

The findings of this survey supports the view that above everything else best bosses understand the needs of their staff, whether to advance their careers in the longer-term or find more immediate satisfactions in the job itself, and they react positively to those needs. As a result many staff in the poll recognise and value the boss's sensitivity to their needs and respond accordingly.

> 'He helped me identify and use skills I didn't think I had.'

> 'As a result of his management style I am much more committed to my work. In other jobs I got bored easily, but with my present boss my enthusiasm is high. In other jobs I expressed ideas but felt I was wasting my time.'

The notion of developing each person's unique capabilities as a way of guiding them towards greater performance relates in many ways to the principle of empowerment – encouraging staff to see beyond their own expectations of themselves. Whether through a sensitivity to what motivates individual staff, setting stretch goals, giving them frequent feedback and recognition, permitting individuals to run with their own ideas and trusting them to do their best, it seems that good bosses get more out of their staff by creating the conditions in which they can get the best out of themselves.

> *A case example from the article 'What Great Managers Do' relates the experience of one store manager in the Walgreen chain. In most of the thousand stores a simple structure exists in which each employee owns an aisle where they are not only responsible for serving customers but for keeping the aisle clean, tagging items and carrying out stock revisions as new stock is introduced and old stock replaced. The arrangement is simple and efficient and gives each employee broad responsibility.*
>
> *Faced with a situation where she had one employee who was particularly good with customers and another who didn't enjoy interacting with customers but had great analytical skills the manager went to some lengths to accommodate both sets of needs by modifying their roles. As a result one took on more of a merchandising and sales role while the other assumed broader responsibilities for handling major resets and aspects of the manager's functions, which is where their interests lay for the future.*
>
> *As each individual's skills and confidence grew the store manager was ever conscious of the need to keep redesigning their work and roles to stretch them even further, but always with a view to fitting the challenges to their unique attributes and needs rather than trying to fit the person into a standard role.*

While the tactics employed by good bosses provide rich lessons for other managers they also have a profound effect on many staff

What Real Delegators Do

who identify them as the person who singularly drew out their talents and helped them access career opportunities. Recognising them as seeing a potential they often failed to recognise in themselves, many commented that this manager was the first person to identify their latent capabilities and use them in the most productive ways.

> 'My present boss has been able to get the most out of me. He helped me show my true potential and allowed me to grow. The results have been mutually beneficial.'

In return for being given opportunities to realise their potential a significant number of survey respondents used similar language in commenting that as a result they were prepared to 'go the extra mile' and 'pull out all the stops' for their boss when the occasion demanded. In one case when asked what their best boss had gained from them that other bosses hadn't, the reply was,

> 'Everything! My complete loyalty and willingness to do whatever is asked of me in my role, regardless of where or when. My loyalty goes beyond the demands of the job and I have the utmost respect and support from my boss in return.'

The most common outcome from having a good boss seems to be commitment and loyalty, in action as well as words. Bringing out the best in others usually means that staff in turn strive to deliver the best possible performance for their boss. And while the knock-on effects in staff retention and increased productivity are difficult to quantify there is a sense that having a good boss is not only profoundly developmental but has lasting effect in stimulating the desire to take responsibility, seek career advancement and develop important skills in working with others.

AND WORST BOSSES TOO

While they may learn a great deal from having a good boss many employees also acknowledge the benefits of working with a difficult boss at some stage in their careers. As with strict or controlling parents, whose children often vow to do things differently when bringing up their own children, those who work for intolerable bosses often learn important skills that serve them well in the future. And while they may be seen as worst bosses in some ways, they are also seen as the best in others. During his time at the Ford Motor Company one of Lee Iacocca's staff summed up his style in the following words, 'I never worked for a man I learned more from, admired more – and who is a bigger prick'.

Current CEO of Ryanair Michael O'Leary, hailed as a great entrepreneur by some and as an aggressive and demanding boss by others, reportedly harangues and cajoles his senior staff at Monday meetings to deliver on the most stretching of targets for the week. 'Nobody misses them for fear of being savaged – if you argue back you get your head kicked in', said one senior executive who has since left the company. But while he is often portrayed as a bully and control freak he is also credited with great ability when it comes to motivating staff and keeping them focused on the end result (to run a super-efficient airline). While playing to their individual strengths he wholeheartedly backs up his staff when they are challenged, and if he trusts people he lets them take complete control – 'once he trusts you, you can do what you want – the biggest sin is to do nothing', comments one of his senior staff. As a result he does not expect his staff to raise problems unless they also have solutions – 'you don't start something and expect him to fix it' warns one of the crew. However, in the same way that commentators fear should O'Leary leave the company it would be in danger of collapse, worst bosses run the risk of losing good people to other organisations where the pace is less frenetic and their efforts are better appreciated.[6]

What Real Delegators Do

In the final analysis, it seems that whether working for a good or a bad boss, a symbiotic relationship often develops where both sides get what they need from the relationship, the boss to achieve results or broaden their influence, and the staff to be stretched, learn, get promotion or be pushed into action. And there is often an indefinable synergy in the relationship between a powerful boss and their staff based on mutual respect or healthy tension that leads to better results than could be achieved from working separately. In the same way that creative and spontaneous bosses are often held in check by an able financial controller or operations manager putting the brakes on his or her ambitions, so good and bad bosses are frequently complemented by a responsible and committed workforce.

Delegation is about letting go of real responsibility to others and trusting them to give of their best, a critical part of the management job and one where many run into difficulties. Though they may espouse otherwise, the human condition is that most managers don't let go easily to others and they certainly don't let go to people they don't trust. Developing a level of trust sufficient to confidently let go requires managers to start with themselves. Unless you know what you want to achieve as a manager and are giving time to those challenges it is hard to let go to others. And if you don't let go you will never get to trust your staff. Many managers, who identify a need to reduce the amount of time they spend on day-to-day routine and urgency in order to concentrate on the real job of work, find themselves trapped in a cycle of mistrust that inexorably leads to closer control, less responsible staff and even tighter controls.

Reversing the tendency to hang on to aspects of the job they should be letting go of to others requires managers to make more quality time for staff, to clarify what is required, coach them in taking on new challenges, monitor what they give away and recognise them for their contribution. If you are currently putting in long hours, with a less-than-committed workforce, or feel that in your absence the work wouldn't get done to your satisfaction then consider doing some things differently. On the basis that if what you are doing now isn't working one option is to try something else. Start in small ways to reverse the self-fulfilling prophesy where you end up doing certain tasks because it is easier and quicker, and your staff become irresponsible as they sense an increasing mistrust from their manager or a style of management that does not allow them to grow. Simple options for doing things differently may include some of the following:

1. Carry out an annual review of your role and the way you are currently dividing your time.
2. Involve your key staff in suggesting ways you could let go more of your work.
3. Use your Diary to block out chunks of time for your priorities and projects.
4. Let your staff know your priorities for the day or week so they can assist and support you.
5. Schedule time in the week for MBWA.
6. Reduce your availability – have a quiet time in the day or week when you are not prepared to be interrupted.
7. Get into the habit of pushing problems back by asking people for options and solutions.
8. Re-clarify the roles and responsibilities of your staff annually.
9. Invite staff who may feel they are overloaded, working long hours or under-performing to carry out a time log exercise on themselves.
10. Start to keep a prioritised To Do List or Weekly Planner and get your staff to do the same.
11. Draw up a responsibility chart for the Department indicating who is responsible for what.
12. Institute regular daily or weekly meetings with your staff as a way of minimising ad hoc interruptions.

13. Commit to carrying out quarterly reviews and goal-setting – encourage your staff to identify challenges in the job and coach them on making progress.
14. Keep an ongoing record of the feedback you want to give individuals and let them know frequently how they are doing.
15. Build more individual recognition into staff meetings and plan events for celebrating group successes.
16. Work on difficult staff. Confront them about behavioural or performance problems.
17. Repeat more frequently what you want/don't want from particular staff.
18. Do an annual training plan to identify the skill gaps and aspirations of your staff.
19. Find more creative ways to recognise people for good work.
20. Agree deadlines with staff for finishing longer-term tasks or parts of projects.
21. Carry out a periodic climate or attitude survey and set up a task group to manage areas of shortfall.
22. Plan to do a bit more casual listening to your staff.

Although managers aspire to getting the best out of their staff there is often a gap between what they espouse and what they deliver. External pressures to respond to the more immediate demands of the day often means that things which are important but less urgent, such as following up on delegated tasks or having regular one-on-ones, get consigned to a growing list of things to get done. Ensuring that real delegation is more than an aspiration means institutionalising some activities as part of your day, week and month. Start by scheduling more time for your own priorities, which includes the longer-term goals and daily priorities that need to be managed differently from the urgency and routine that can so easily drive the day. Use your Diary to block out an hour or two each week for planning or thinking and get into the habit of using a To Do List or Weekly

Planner to schedule for short-term tasks that will move you in the direction of your longer-term challenges and goals.

Also find ways to commit quality time to your staff, whether for quarterly job reviews, weekly team meetings or casual wandering around; and don't allow those commitments to become casualties to the passing needs of the day. In structuring your day and week also consider the way in which people take on major responsibilities in their lives, whether buying a house, building a boat or going back to study. When they are clear about what they need to do, have the support and assistance of others and are recognised for their achievements, most staff are only too willing to take on new challenges and learn from them. Not alone for your benefit but in the interest of getting the best out of your people, letting go of some things is truly a function of hanging on to others.

References

Chapter 1

1. Bennis, W. (1976), *The Unconscious Conspiracy: Why Leaders Can't Lead*, New York, NY: AMACOM.
2. Peters, T. and Waterman, R.H. (1982), *In Search of Excellence: Lessons from America's Best Run Companies*, New York, NY: Harper and Row.
3. Collins, J.C. and Porras, J.I. (1996), *Built to Last: Successful Habits of Visionary Companies*, London: Century House.
4. Pascale, R.T. (1990), *Managing on the Edge*, New York, NY: Random House.
5. Drucker, P. (1967), *The Effective Executive*, London: Pan Books, p. 31.
6. Argyris, C. (1998), 'Empowerment: The Emperor's New Clothes', *Harvard Business Review*, May–June.
7. Marshall (1986), 'A Survey of Differences in Communication Between Managers and Subordinates', *Leadership and Organisational Development Journal*.
8. Kanter, R.M. (1993), *The Change Masters*, New York, NY: Simon and Schuster.

Chapter 2

1. Reps, P. and Senzaki, N. (1978), *Zen Flesh, Zen Bones*, Doubleday.
2. Mintzberg, H. (1973), *The Nature of Managerial Work*, New York, NY: Harper & Row.
3. Hersey, P. and Blanchard, K.H. (1982), *Management of Organizational Behavior: Utilising Human Resources*, Englewood Cliffs, NJ: Prentice-Hall.

4. Sant, R.W., Bakke, D. and Wetlaufer, W. (1999), 'Organising for Empowerment: An Interview with Roger Sant and Dennis Bakke', *Harvard Business Review*, Jan.

Chapter 3

1. Iacocca, L. and Novak, W. (1984), *Iacocca: A Biography*, New York, NY: Bantam Books.
2. Becker, L.J. (1978), 'Joint Effect of Feedback and Goal Setting On Performance: A Field Study of Residential Energy Consumption', *Journal of Applied Psychology*, Vol. 63, No. 4, pp. 428–433.
3. Latham, G.P. and Locke, E.A. (1979), 'Goal Setting—A Motivational Technique that Works', *Organizational Dynamics*, Autumn, Vol. 8, No. 2, pp. 68–80.
4. Maltz, M. (1960), *Psycho-Cybernetics*, Englewood Cliffs, NJ: Prentice-Hall.

Chapter 4

1. Rogers, C.R. and Roethlisberger, F.J. (1991), 'Barriers and Gateways to Communication', *Harvard Business Review*, Nov.
2. Zuker, E. (1991), *The Seven Secrets of Influence*, New York, NY: McGraw-Hill.
3. Goleman, D. (1998), *Working with Emotional Intelligence*, London: Bloomsbury.
4. Welch, J. and Byrne, J.A. (2001), *Jack: What I've Learned Leading a Great Company and Great People*, London: Headline.
5. Oncken, W. and Wass, D.L. (1999), 'Management Time: Who's got the Monkey?', *Harvard Business Review*, Nov–Dec.

Chapter 5

1. Oswald, A. (2001) study referenced in '50 Best Companies to Work For', *Sunday Times*.

References

2. Maslow, A.H. (1943), 'A Theory of Human Motivation', *Psychological Review*, Vol. 50, No. 4, July, pp. 370–396.
3. Kovach, K.A. (1987), 'What Motivates Employees? Workers and Supervisors Give Different Answers', *Business Horizons*, Vol. 50, No. 5, September–October, pp 58–65.
4. Herzberg, F. (1987), 'One More Time: How Do You Motivate Employees?', *Harvard Business Review*, September–October, pp. 109–119.
5. Myers, M.S. (1970), *Every Employee a Manager*, New York, NY: McGraw-Hill.
6. Rosenthal, R. and Jacobson, L. (1968), *Pygmalion in the Classroom*, New York, NY: Holt, Reinhart and Winston, Inc.
7. Livingston, J.S. (1988), 'Pygmalion in Management', *Harvard Business Review*, September–October, pp. 121–130.
8. Zander, R.S. and Zander, B. (2000), *The Art of Possibility: Transforming Professional and Personal Life*, Boston, MA: Harvard Business School.
9. Levinson, H. (1970), 'Management by Whose Objectives', *Harvard Business Review Classic*.
10. Argyris, C. (1985), *Strategy, Change and Defensive Routines*, Boston, MA: Pitman.

Chapter 6

1. Adapted from Weisbord, M. (1976), 'Organizational Diagnosis, Six Places to Look for Trouble with or without a Theory', *Group and Organizational Studies*, Vol. 1, No. 4, pp. 430–447.
2. Belbin, R.M. (1981), *Management Teams*, Oxford: Butterworth-Heinemann.
3. Luft, J. and Ingham, H. (1955), 'The Johari Window, a Graphic Model of Interpersonal Awareness', *Proceedings of the Western Training Laboratory in Group Development*, Los Angeles, CA: UCLA.
4. Janis, I. (1972), *Groupthink: Psychological Studies of Policy Decisions and Fiascos*, New York, NY: Houghton Mifflin.

5. Harvey, J.R. (1988), *The Abilene Paradox and Other Mediations on Management*, Lexington, MA: Lexington Books.
6. McConalogue, T. (2003), 'The Four P's of Productive Meetings', *Education*, March, pp. 15–17.

Chapter 7

1. Maltz, M. (1960), *Psycho-Cybernetics*, Englewood Cliffs, NJ: Prentice-Hall.
2. Lundin, S.C., Paul, H. and Christensen, J. (2000), *Fish!: A Remarkable Way to Boost Morale and Improve Results*, London: Hodder and Stoughton.

Chapter 8

1. McConalogue, T. (2003), *Eat the Elephants and Fight the Ants: How to Take More Control of Your Time*, Dublin: Blackhall Publishing.
2. Peters, T. and Waterman, R.H. (1982), *In Search of Excellence: Lessons from America's Best Run Companies*, New York, NY: Harper and Row.

Chapter 9

1. Survey carried out by IrishJobs.ie and reported in the *Irish Independent* by Martha Kearns, 16 November 2004.
2. Larkin, T.J. (1994), *Communicating Change: How to Win Employee Support for New Business Directions*, New York, NY: McGraw-Hill.
3. Goffee, R. and Jones. G. (2000), 'Why Should Anyone be Led by You?', *Harvard Business Review*, September–October, pp. 63–69.
4. Blanchard, K. and Johnson, S. (1983), *The One Minute Manager*, London: Willow Books.
5. Buckingham, M. (2005), 'What Great Managers Do', *Harvard Business Review*, Vol. 83, No. 3, March.
6. Creaton, S. (2004), *Ryanair: How a Small Irish Airline Conquered Europe*, Dublin: Aurum Press.